"I am so happy to endorse Darlene's new book, *The Golden Thread*. For me, Darlene has constantly been an example of pursuing the presence of God. She is the kind of person I want to hear from when it comes to the highs and lows of life's journey. Darlene is a trusted voice. She runs after the heart of God. I know your faith will be lifted and increased with this new treasure."

—Chris Tomlin

"This book is such a gift to us all. We still tend to think that bad things do not happen to great people. But here is the story of a great person afflicted by illness and yet who still manages to keep singing. When you see Darlene leading worship it's really only a small glimpse into the reservoir of faith and passion she has for her God and for people. She is a great mom and grand mom, devoted wife, local pastor, and lifelong friend. All her dreams are about the presence of God impacting people and this book will give us all more insight into how dedicated she is to seeing that."

—Martin and Anna Smith

PRAISE FOR *THE GOLDEN THREAD*

"Our Mum is a stunning example of how fulfilling life can be when you align yourself fully with the Word of God. Within the pages of this book lies God's perfect plan and purpose for your future and a constant reminder of just how much you are loved. Even through the very tough seasons and challenging days, she has always displayed a resilience to live and breathe the Spirit of God, as is evidenced throughout each page of this anointed book. May this book encourage you to seek God in a deeper way, and to trust Him with your storms, your battles, your families, and your future."

—Andrew, Amy, Ava Pearl, Roman
Emmanuel, and Ruthie Feather

"When it comes to being a carrier of the presence of God, we see Mum as one who does this with pure grace. It is no wonder that she pioneered and paved a way for people to experience God in all His fullness through worship. This book not only speaks to the heart of who she is and how she lives her life, but also to the moments when we sometimes find it hard to find hope. We believe that this book will not only bless you, but also empower you to live a life that is fully surrendered to Jesus and allow the Holy Spirit to do a new thing in you."

—Chloe and Hosanna (and Thea)

"My amazing mum has made the presence of God so normal for us as we keep learning to welcome the Holy Spirit into every part of our lives. I love that as we worship and as we keep lifting Jesus above everything else, His presence, which is really just like heaven on earth, becomes the one thing that defines us as a person and the one thing that defines our identity. Not only is she just an incredible pioneer in worship but she is a great mum and truly loves her children, grandkids, husband, and friends. So we thank you, Mum, for everything you do for us and I really hope this book blesses lots of people."

—Love, Zoe Jewel

THE
GOLDEN
THREAD

THE
GOLDEN
THREAD

EXPERIENCING GOD'S PRESENCE
IN EVERY SEASON OF LIFE

DARLENE
ZSCHECH

EMANATE
BOOKS

Published in Nashville, Tennessee, by Emanate Books, an imprint of Thomas Nelson. Emanate Books and Thomas Nelson are registered trademarks of HarperCollins Christian Publishing, Inc.

Published in association with the literary agency Iconic Media Brands LLC.

Thomas Nelson titles may be purchased in bulk for educational, business, fund-raising, or sales promotional use. For information, please e-mail SpecialMarkets@ThomasNelson.com.

Scripture quotations marked AMP are from the Amplified® Bible. Copyright © 1954, 1958, 1962, 1964, 1965, 1987 by The Lockman Foundation. Used by permission. (www.Lockman.org)

Scripture quotations marked AMPC are from the Amplified Bible, Classic Edition. Copyright © 1954, 1958, 1962, 1964, 1965, 1987 by The Lockman Foundation. Used by permission. (www.Lockman.org)

Scripture quotations marked THE MESSAGE are from *The Message*. Copyright © by Eugene H. Peterson 1993, 1994, 1995, 1996, 2000, 2001, 2002. Used by permission of NavPress. All rights reserved. Represented by Tyndale House Publishers, Inc.

Scripture quotations marked NASB are from New American Standard Bible®. Copyright © 1960, 1962, 1963, 1968, 1971, 1972, 1973, 1975, 1977, 1995 by The Lockman Foundation. Used by permission. (www.Lockman.org)

Scripture quotations marked NIV are from the Holy Bible, New International Version®, NIV®. Copyright © 1973, 1978, 1984, 2011 by Biblica, Inc.® Used by permission of Zondervan. All rights reserved worldwide. www.Zondervan.com. The "NIV" and "New International Version" are trademarks registered in the United States Patent and Trademark Office by Biblica, Inc.®

Scripture quotations marked NKJV are from the New King James Version®. © 1982 by Thom-as Nelson. Used by permission. All rights reserved.

Scripture quotations marked NLT are from the Holy Bible, New Living Translation. © 1996, 2004, 2007, 2013, 2015 by Tyndale House Foundation. Used by permission of Tyndale House Publishers, Inc., Carol Stream, Illinois 60188. All rights reserved.

Scripture quotations marked TPT are from The Passion Translation®. Copyright © 2017, 2018 by Passion & Fire Ministries, Inc. Used by permission. All rights reserved. ThePassionTransla-tion.com.

Scripture quotations marked ESV are from the ESV® Bible (The Holy Bible, English Standard Version®). Copyright © 2001 by Crossway, a publishing ministry of Good News Publishers. Used by permission. All rights reserved.

Scripture quotations marked GNT are from the Good News Translation in Today's English Version—Second Edition. Copyright 1992 by American Bible Society. Used by permission.

Scripture quotations marked KJV are from the King James Version. Public domain.

ISBN 978-0-7852-1954-5 (eBook)
ISBN 978-0-7852-1953-8 (HC)
ISBN 978 0 7852 2199 9 (IE)

Library of Congress Control Number: 2018949214

Printed in the United States of America

18 19 20 21 22 LSC 10 9 8 7 6 5 4 3 2 1

CONTENTS

CONTENTS

FOREWORD

DARLENE IS AN AMAZING WORSHIP LEADER, BUT MORE THAN THAT, she is an amazing person. I have had the privilege of knowing her for more than twenty years now, and I can say that in all of that time I have never seen her behave in any way that was not in accord with the character of Jesus. She has known tragedy like most of us, and even in those times she has navigated her circumstances with grace while continuing to minister to others.

Darlene's extensive experience as a worship leader has led her along an amazing journey of personal growth in her relationship with God. It's made her passionate about helping others realize the awesome potential we all have in Christ to live a life of worship that honors God and brings the influence of His kingdom into the world around us.

In *The Golden Thread*, she does a marvelous job of sharing how we can see the continual thread of God's love, mercy, and goodness all throughout our lives, both in the good times and the hard ones. And she knows about this from personal experience. Her private battle with cancer was horrendous, and yet she continued to trust God throughout the struggle and is now enjoying the results of His healing power.

This book will encourage anyone who is going through their own private battle with disappointment, fear, sickness, or any other painful event in life. As one who has gone through tragedy and made it safely to the other side, Darlene will inspire you to go deeper in your faith and have greater intimacy with God.

If life is good for you right now, the book will reaffirm the goodness of God to you and strengthen your faith even more, equipping you to do whatever you need to do in life.

Darlene is one of those rare people who makes a deposit into every life she touches. So whatever your situation may be, her message will give you a stronger hunger and thirst for God—to live every day in His presence.

As you read this book, I pray that you will be touched by her beautiful spirit and that you will find healing for your own pain.

I am glad that I have had Darlene in my life, and when I am with her I am always challenged to love God more!

June 14, 2018

Joyce Meyer

NOTE FROM
MARK ZSCHECH

At her heart, my wife, Darlene, is a worshipper. I can tell you she is always chasing God's presence. She makes her passion for the presence of Jesus her daily pursuit. That's why I am so proud of her for writing *The Golden Thread*. The overriding theme of this book is the beauty of God's presence woven throughout our lives.

Throughout our lives there are many "threads" that make up our personal tapestries. But what if we adjusted our view of this statement just a bit? What if, instead, we say a collection of stories woven together makes one beautiful rug? Where my story becomes our story, which represents His story.

Recently friends showed us the Japanese art of Kintsugi. This is a repair method that celebrates and emphasizes the beauty of broken, historic pottery pieces. Instead of hiding or disguising the damage, the Japanese repair these vessels with threads of real gold, making the repaired piece of art even more beautiful than the original. The golden thread has given broken pieces of ceramic new life.

Isn't that what God does with our lives? Even with all the twists and turns we face, God still manages to make a beautiful piece of art of our journey.

Darlene is going to transport you—it's a relocation program of the nice kind—to a place where you are reminded and encouraged to think of a more glorious way of describing God's handiwork in your life. A place where, no matter what's broken or cracked, God gives you beauty for ashes and it becomes your golden thread.

Our family truly prays that this book becomes a blessing to you and that it strengthens you in your story. Remember, your ending is not yet written.

Mark Zschech
Hope Unlimited Church
164 Pacific HWY, Charmhaven,
New South Wales
Australia

INTRODUCTION

DISCOVERING THE GOLDEN THREAD

As one who was wonderfully and radically converted by the love of Jesus Christ in my teenage years, I can look back over my life and see the faithfulness of God woven throughout every day—like a pure golden thread of His love and His nature.

If you have heard any part of my story at all, you already know how the love of God changed my life and continues to gently transform me. His presence not only fills me with gratitude and wonder but also points me to the reality of the glory of God and His kindness, while even in my toughest moments, lovingly drawing me to experience Him in deeper ways.

I've followed Jesus for many years now, but to be honest His love for me still catches me by surprise. I continually encounter glimpses of an unexpected Holy as I see His relentless pursuit of my heart, the Holy Spirit leading me to a place of hiddenness in Christ and a trust in His character that has brought me much peace. Whether you are in the easiest of times or the hardest of times, God is always with us. He is where I place all my confident hope. He is the One who made a way for each of us and the One who continues to love us and be fully present in each of our lives.

The prophet Isaiah spoke of the days in which we are living today as growing darker but the light of Christ and His glory shining ever brighter in our world (Isaiah 60). The contrast between the darkening times we are experiencing and the Light of the World who is ever-present with us will only become more and more visible as we draw closer to the day of the great return of Christ. But until that day, no matter what goes on around us, we can be fully confident that God is with us.

He is not angry with us. In fact, when we open our hearts to His love, we will find that, just as the woman at the well in the Scriptures discovered, Jesus is ready and willing to reach out to us and meet not only our physical needs but also quench our spiritual thirst (John 4). She encountered the unexpected Holy in her meeting with Jesus and encountered His presence and love in such a transforming way that she went forth and shared His love with whoever would listen.

God's golden thread of mercy continues to weave its way throughout each of our days and our lives in ways that are both mysterious and yet easy to see as He draws humanity toward Himself. I experienced this afresh in the journey that our family was about to embark upon . . . a journey of brilliant new beginnings and of personal crisis.

A SPECIAL PLACE FOR MY BELOVED

My dear friend Sue is a great prayer warrior at our church. She sends my husband, Mark, and me—and many other people—amazing prophetic words to encourage us along our journeys. I know she hears from God, for she heard Him whisper the following words for me. She wrote this *before* I had shared with her that I had been diagnosed with cancer; she knew she was to write a book full of scripture about His love for me:

> As God takes you to His special place, reserved just for you and for Him, may you be blessed beyond your wildest dreams. "Like an apple tree [rare and welcome] among the trees of the forest, so is my beloved among the young men! He has brought me to his banqueting place, and his banner over me is love [waving overhead to protect and comfort me]. Sustain me with raisin cakes, refresh me with apples, because I am sick with love. Let his left hand be under my head and his right hand embrace me." My beloved speaks and says to me, 'Arise, my love, my fair one, and come away!'" (Song of Songs 2:3–6, 10 AMP) This sums up what is in His heart for you on your upcoming journey. Simply rest in Him, for in this is the key to your healing. This is the key to life and all that it entails.

I deeply treasured this word from Sue and could feel God's heart of love as she spoke of my healing. I have held onto those words closely. I especially needed them as I entered into a new season of my life, a season I had never imagined and was not ready for. After a diagnosis of cancer in my body, many people around me panicked—and I must admit that I panicked too. But Sue's note and consequent pages she lovingly wrote—sharing words from the heart of God—reminded me of the golden thread of God's unfailing love toward me. I may have been unprepared, but He was making a way for me all along. My trust in God and His promises allowed me to rest and hope in a name greater than any diagnosis and just bury my face into the chest of my Beloved, the place in my world where all pain, fear, and doubt were not invited to enter, and where His love poured into me like a rushing waterfall of security. It was the moment of my unexpected Holy. The golden thread of love and mercy had entwined itself around me yet again.

Never in all my wildest dreams did I anticipate the depth of empathy and love that flowed straight from God's heart into the very core of my physical being, where I felt it in every cell of my body. And even with all the wonderful help I received from my dearest friends and family, and with all the amazing medical care and advice that I gained from my team of doctors and specialists, the warmth of God's words to my heart was what really reached me in my time of need.

"I will lead you on the right path," He said to me. "I will make the way plain for you to follow."

Those are the words that I have since clung to again and again. When post-chemo pain rises up in my body or I have a little emotional wobble, I have had to discipline myself to go straight back to His loving words over my life.

THE BEGINNING OF GOD'S GOLDEN THREAD OF GRACE

God's grace has been ever-present in this world since the very beginning, the dawning of Creation. When God said, "Let there be light," then Light appeared to guide us (Genesis 1). Even after the fall of Adam and Eve in the garden of Eden, when they chose to follow their own will and their own way rather than God's, a plan of restoration had already been set in motion (Genesis 3). The golden thread of grace was present even in Jesus, who is the Lamb of God slain *before* the foundation of the world (Revelation 13:8). And not only has God's grace been present in this world since the beginning of time, but it has been present in your life, available to you for all that you need, since before you were born.

But just as Adam and Eve turned away from the grace and the love of God so long ago, we also do the same. We lose sight of the golden thread of grace when our eyes and our ears turn away from

God, and we begin to look and listen to the voices of the world around us. Ultimately, anything that draws our attention and affection away from the Lord of all creation has been orchestrated by the one who loves to deceive and to destroy anything good in this world or in our lives.

Back in the day of Creation, God called your name, just as He called out to Adam and Eve after they had sinned, to draw them back to Himself. He called to you while you were still in your mother's womb, as He fearfully and wonderfully formed you before you were ever born (Psalm 139:14). God called you when you were still an enemy of His, wooing you back to His grace and His love. God calls you still today, to enter His presence, to practice His presence, to live every moment with Him in mind, through every season of your life.

HE IS GOOD!

My hope and prayer is that this book will help bring a calm to your storm, hope to your own doubts, and love to your own fears, because there is not one of us who is immune to seasons that challenge us and stretch us beyond what we feel we can bear. But neither is there one of us who is exempt from the love of God that flows toward us, no matter what opposition we are facing, no matter what season of life we find ourselves in. It is true that there are some things about God and how He is at work in the world and in us that we will never really understand until we have come to the end of ourselves. But the greatest thing we all need to remember about our God is that *He is good*.

May you be encouraged as you read *The Golden Thread*, and may the sweet Holy Spirit nudge you along the way to help you understand the love and grace He has for you in the season you are walking in right now.

Take hold of the golden thread of His Presence, His loving kindness, His goodness, His power, and His grace as you read the following pages.

Your friend on the journey,
Darlene Zschech

THE GOLDEN SECRET

PSALM 16

A precious song, engraved in gold, by King David

Keep me safe, O mighty God.
    I run for dear life to you, my safe place.
So I said to the Lord God,
"You are my Maker, my Mediator, and my Master.
    Any good thing you find in me has come from
        you."
And he said to me, "My holy lovers are wonderful,
    my majestic ones, my glorious ones,
    fulfilling all my desires."
Yet there are those who yield to their weakness,
    and they will have troubles and sorrows
        unending.
    I never gather with such ones,
    nor give them honor in any way.
Lord, I have chosen you alone as my inheritance.
    You are my prize, my pleasure, and my
        portion.

I leave my destiny and its timing in your hands.
Your pleasant path leads me to pleasant places.
    I'm overwhelmed by the privileges
    that come with following you,
    for you have given me the best!
The way you counsel and correct me makes me
    praise you more,
    for your whispers in the night give me wisdom,
    showing me what to do next.
Because you are close to me and always available,
    my confidence will never be shaken,
    for I experience your wrap-around presence
    every moment.
My heart and soul explode with joy—full of glory!
    Even my body will rest confident and secure.
For you will not abandon me to the realm of death,
    nor will you allow your Holy One to
    experience corruption.
For you bring me a continual revelation of
    resurrection life,
    the path to the bliss that brings me face-to-
    face with you. (TPT)

GOD'S PRESENCE
IS EVERYTHING

The Christian life is to live all of your
life in the presence of God.
—R. C. SPROUL, FROM "PLEASING GOD"

I WAS FIFTEEN YEARS OF AGE WHEN I HAD MY FIRST REAL AND personal encounter with God. It was a moment that changed everything as my heart said *yes* to the golden thread of the Holy Spirit's work of love and mercy in my life. I had sensed the presence of God many times growing up. My grandparents had been in church since they were kids, and they had led our family in the same way, and my parents were involved in serving others through various mission endeavors in my formative years. So, to be around the house of God and the people of God was not new to me. But to encounter Him *for myself*, one evening at a youth meeting when I asked Jesus to be the center of my world, immediately and radically changed me.

It was during this season, for which I will always be grateful, that the love of God overwhelmed me and wiped the slate of my heart clean. To serve Him completely was my immediate response. I now understand that when I became a Christian, I accepted the Father, the Son, and the Holy Spirit—all three Persons of God—into my very being. I understood Jesus' sacrifice for me, and I knew that the Holy Spirit had been involved in drawing me to Himself. The Bible tells us that it is the kindness of God that leads us to repentance, and kindness is listed as a fruit of the Spirit, the humbling quality of the Holy Spirit that He used to draw me to Himself. This golden thread of love and mercy has continued to chase me in every season, drawing me back to the Lord over and over again.

A HUNGER FOR MORE

But at the tender age of sixteen, more than a year after I had become a Christian, there was a night at my church when my heart was simply hungry for more of Jesus in my life. I was standing with my youth pastor, who was praying with me and for me. We were asking God to reveal Himself to my heart in a greater dimension than ever before. Suddenly, I found myself speaking in an unknown language, a heavenly language, that was flowing out of my mouth. It was wonderful! But to be honest, as overwhelming as the experience was, it wasn't the only great thing that transpired in my life that evening. That night, I experienced the very real presence of God as never before. Yes, it was wonderful to experience the "unknown tongue," but deep in my soul I encountered an ever-greater revelation of His great love, which I have pursued with eagerness from that day on. Paul's words resonate as I reflect on that experience:

Pursue [this] love [with eagerness, make it your goal], yet earnestly desire and cultivate the spiritual gifts [to be used by believers for the benefit of the church], but especially that you may prophesy [to foretell the future, to speak a new message from God to the people]. For one who speaks in an unknown tongue does not speak to people but to God; for no one understands him or catches his meaning, but by the Spirit he speaks mysteries [secret truths, hidden things]. (1 Corinthians 14:1–2 AMP)

Dear friend, please know that the presence of God is not just a theory; it is the reality of the nearness of the Holy Spirit in our midst! I had already had the miraculous experience of being born again, but that evening, I experienced the power of God's Spirit lighting me up from the inside out. Bit by bit since that time I have continued to find that there is so much more spiritually available to us here on earth than we could possibly imagine! The gift of the Holy Spirit's presence in our lives is experienced in billions of diverse ways by people around the world every moment of every day.

That night at my church, my heart, which had been made alive in Christ at the time of my salvation, was suddenly awakened to another dimension. It is hard for me to describe, but everything and everyone I saw from that moment on just looked more beautiful and, over time, I found myself being able to discern the voice of the Holy Spirit for myself. The Bible became like lyrical poetry to me every time I opened it—almost as if the pages I was reading were in fact reading me. It was so scary and powerful all at the same time!

This experience created a real conundrum of faith within my heart. I wanted more and more of the Lord in my life, but that openness to Him forced me to realize He wanted me to leave more and more of my old self, my old nature, behind. As someone who grew up extremely emotionally needy—this refining can be quite challenging. Still, I found myself compelled to become a part of something greater than myself. I was just sixteen years old, living away from home, and yet I was experiencing a new fire in my belly that I can honestly say is the reason I am still standing here today. The way I explain it is that the Holy Spirit had been *in me*, and now the Holy Spirit was *on me*! His golden thread of love was weaving itself through the fabric of my life in ways I am still only beginning to understand.

The presence of God is such a wonderful gift in our lives, but it can also be easy to take it for granted. I liken it to having a lamp, all ready to go, but if we never access its power, we will never fully see the light that is available to us and we will never experience its benefits in our lives. God's Presence with us here on the earth is a stunning fact, and the raw and powerful dynamic of His Personhood here with us, in our midst, is something that can be difficult at times for us to grasp, especially in the midst of all that we go through in this world. But His love, His acceptance, His voice, His instruction, His warnings, His compassion—*all of Him*, the very essence of who He is to us and through us—is here with us in every moment. I have eagerly desired to welcome the Holy Spirit into my life in deepening ways for many years, and it seems that the more I learn, the hungrier I am for more of His presence in my world.

PRACTICING THE PRESENCE

I so enjoy the presence of my husband. I just like to know he is nearby. Even when he is working away quietly, it is a comfort to know he is near. But it's never enough just to live under the same roof with someone you love. You need time to be *in the moment* together. That's what I began discovering in that singular and remarkable moment when I encountered God's Presence in a powerful and personal way. Yes, God had always been there. He lived inside of me. We were living under the same roof. But my hunger was for more than proximity. I wanted to experience God in His fullness.

The first time I encountered the phrase "practicing the presence" was in a book written by a Carmelite monk named Brother Lawrence. The book, *The Practice of the Presence of God*, is a collection of his teachings gathered and passed down to our modern times from his lifetime in the 1600s.

Brother Lawrence's conversion to Christianity took place when he was eighteen years old:

> In the winter, seeing a tree stripped of its leaves, and considering that within a little time, the leaves would be renewed, and after that the flowers and fruit appear, he received a high view of the Providence and Power of God, which has never since been effaced from his soul.
>
> "I regard myself as the most wretched of all men, stinking and covered with sores, and as one who has committed all sorts of crimes against his King. Overcome by remorse, I confess all my wickedness to Him, ask His pardon and abandon myself entirely to Him to do with as He will. But this King, filled with goodness and mercy, far from chastising me, lovingly embraces me, makes me eat at His table, serves me with His own hands, gives me the keys of His treasures and treats me as His favorite. He talks with me and is delighted with me in a thousand and one ways; He forgives me and relieves me of my principle bad habits without talking about them; I beg Him to make me according to His heart and always the more weak and despicable I see myself to be, the more beloved I am of God."[1]

A life-changing transition took place in Brother Lawrence's life. He spoke of the same kindness that had so gripped and changed my life. His words were a testimony to what had happened to me but also a challenge to actually put into practice a companionship with God that would pervade my life.

This wasn't a hard concept for me. As a musician, I know the value of practice. I have practiced (and still do) musical skills until they have become second nature to me. I no longer have to think through things like I used to do when I was first "practicing."

As I read through Brother Lawrence's prayers and considered his thought processes, I sensed the yearning of his heart, his spirit's desire to be walking totally in step with the Holy Spirit, practicing God's presence every moment of every day. What a wild concept, but what a wonderful revelation and challenge that I have taken to heart, and am still learning.

Receiving the constant and abundant love He has for each of us is what I need to practice more of in my own life: to be still *in Him*—not doing, just being—and allowing Him the freedom to do as He pleases in my life. Not being in control—not having all my ducks in a row—is another dynamic I am learning to embrace in the security of His presence. As someone who is motivated by doing and leading, I can assure you that God's patience with me has been a much needed and delightful blessing.

There are many times in worship that I encounter God's presence so strongly that I sense Him right next to me, speaking to me. I have felt as if my heart would jump right out of my chest. Brother Lawrence teaches about God's "abiding Presence"—experiencing Him in the ordinary moments of life, experiencing Him in the difficult moments of life.

After my cancer diagnosis, while I was going through chemo along with all the fear and uncertainty wrapped up in that experience, I just don't know how I would have been sustained had it not been for the presence of the Holy Spirit. But I have learned that even in the harshest of times, even when God seems silent or distant, as we take the time to lean in and draw close to Him,

He is always whispering His love over us as we make room for the fullness of God's presence in our lives.

ENTERING HIS GATES
THROUGH WORSHIP

There is a great girl in our worship team, sweet Bonnie, who also happens to be an incredible artist. After my crazy season of chemo treatment, she painted an incredible picture of hope for me and my family, which hangs on a wall in our home. It is a picture of a massive storm, with high and treacherous waves all around. But right in the eye of the storm there is calm, and as you look carefully, you'll see a ship with its sails set, sailing on top of the waves and the swell, safe and secure in the midst of raging waters. I am ever reminded of how God delivered me. In any storm of life, the only way to get on the other side of it is to sail right through it. It is God's presence that provides the way.

From my experience, the only safe and sure passage through any storm is to grab hold of His promises like an anchor and worship your heart out until you actually believe what you are declaring! The golden thread of His presence and the practice of it daily is an intentional stance of faith. You enter the gates of heaven through thanksgiving and praise.

Yet, grasping and trusting His presence is not always an easy thing to do. As one who loves to have all (well, at least most) things in order, it can be a helpless feeling to find the only answer to facing a challenge is not to work harder but to simply love and trust through worship. It can feel like a weakness. But over the years as God has shown Himself unwavering in His love and devotion to me, watching Him take my weakness and shine through it with His strength is part of His greater glory in my life.

When we enter His gates through worship, we invite Him to

walk with us and to carry us through every storm we face. At times I am calm and grateful, at other times I am voiceless and desperate. But God's goodness toward me as He draws near remains the same. My friend and author Alicia Britt Chole says this: "To worship in the light is a joy-filled act of faith. To worship in the dark is a faith-fueled act of war."[2]

The storms of life will come, but it's how we respond that will eventually reveal the extent of the damage—and His deliverance. In my heart I know I want to stand and declare as Moses did in the wilderness:

> If your presence doesn't take the lead here, call this trip off right now. How else will it be known that you're with me in this, with me and your people? Are you traveling with us or not? How else will we know that we're special, I and your people, among all other people on this planet Earth? (Exodus 33:15 THE MESSAGE)

God will be with us in the greatest of times, but oh, He is with us in the worst of times too! It doesn't matter what the situation is that I face. I am *always* free to be filled with joy despite the pressures of this life. The Lord our God is in our midst. He takes great delight in you, He renews you by His love, and He shouts for joy over you (Zephaniah 3:17)! So, worship Him. Sing your praises to His name! With the psalmist, declare these words:

> But as for me, I will sing about your power. Each morning I will sing with joy about your unfailing love. For you have been my refuge, a place of safety when I am in distress. O my Strength, to you I sing praises, for you, O God, are my refuge, the God who shows me unfailing love. (Psalm 59:16–17 NLT)

Our worship should always be our response to His majesty, our tribute to God when He shows up in our lives, the created responding to the Creator, our spirits being fueled in His presence as we invite the Giver of life to do in us what only He can do.

SING A SONG!

Songs of worship are a gift that gives us words and melodies to scrape our hearts off the floor and point them heavenward. You don't have to be a musician or have a wonderful voice to experience God's presence through songs of worship. All you need is a heart after God.

> The words and melody of songs will help you to . . .
> Express the true faith that is already in your heart;
> Shout above the distracting and sometimes negative noise in
> your life;
> Focus your eyes and thoughts on what is lovely and true;
> Experience a supernatural joy in the midst of hardship;
> Lift up Jesus, the goal of our worship.

All of us, as worshippers of this living, loving, accepting, life-changing, kind, and all-knowing God, are called to bring our lives before Him as a spiritual act of worship (Romans 12:1). He is not after our performance. He is after our hearts. That's it. But here's the most wonderful result of a worshipful life. When you begin to declare the song of your heart, when you begin to announce the faithfulness of God at every turn of your life, when you bring even a mustard seed of faith to your melody, when all you can do is whisper as you sing, "I give thanks to the Lord for His steadfast love endures forever," you, like King Jehoshaphat (2 Chronicles 20), will stand and watch the Lord Himself ambush satan with your song. Your song of worship is your bold statement of faith—and you will not fall! When His presence is made manifest in our midst, we are safe and secure in the harbor of His goodness.

KEEP PURSUING

If you find yourself casually meandering through worship, getting distracted or maybe even a little sleepy (which happens to us all), just keep pursuing Jesus. Make the time and set aside a place where it's all about you and Him. He is not hard to find. Sometimes all it takes is a bit of tenacity on our part to respond and simply say, "In this moment, it's only You and me." Then wait and be ready for Him to speak. I promise you, He will.

If you have seasons of doubt, you're not alone. Even David, the man after God's own heart, wondered if God was hiding from him. But his hunger for God's presence would not allow him to give up.

Lord, when you said to me, "Seek my face," my inner being responded, "I'm seeking your face with all my heart." So don't hide yourself, Lord, when I come to find you. You're the God of my salvation; how can you reject your servant in anger? You've been my only hope, so don't forsake me now when I need you! My father and mother abandoned me. I'm like an orphan! But you took me in and made me yours. (Psalm 27:8–10 TPT)

WHEN WE WORSHIP

- When we worship Jesus, we declare His kingdom come and we announce His presence on the earth.
- When we worship the Lord, we are coming to Him by faith, bringing the voice of our hearts before heaven.
- When we worship God, we are dispelling the darkness and taking authority over every principality and power that would try to defy and delay God's work in the earth.
- When we worship, we are exalting Christ and His dominion over every situation and circumstance.

- When we worship through the power of the Holy Spirit, thanksgiving is our entry point, joy is our strength, and breakthrough is our inheritance.
- When we worship, the demons tremble and the angels join in.
- When we worship, God's kingdom dominion is established in our lives.

Whatever you are facing today, grab hold of the golden thread of God's faithfulness. Make time to enter into His presence. Make room for His Word and His Spirit to speak to you and encourage you. Practice the presence of God in every situation, every circumstance you encounter, and allow Him to move through you as you feel His delight and His joy in you, His beloved child.

2

SEEK HIM FIRST

*The key to Christian living is a thirst and
hunger for God. And one of the main reasons
people do not understand or experience the
sovereignty of grace and the way it works
through the awakening of sovereign joy is that
their hunger and thirst for God is so small.*
—JOHN PIPER

HAVE YOU EVER BEEN SO PHYSICALLY THIRSTY THAT EVEN THOUGH
you kept drinking water, it just didn't seem to satisfy? Some of the
summers here in Australia can be so humid and hot that it seems
nothing can satisfy your longing for a long, cool drink. This is also
when most Aussies get to the ocean as soon as they can to fully
immerse themselves in the sea.

Welcome to the searching heart of the woman at the well before she encountered Jesus (John 4). My heart has always gone out to this woman, so desperate to belong that she obviously had made a string of poor choices regarding her relationships. Her soul had searched and searched, but she continued to come up short in matters of the heart.

In seasons of transition, we often find ourselves looking for something to fill the hole that changes in our lives seem to create. It's like trying to find a sure footing in the shifting sands, incredibly exhausting and never satisfying. The thirsty and tired woman at the well already knew for certain that a Savior was on the way. She had no idea how or where or when He would appear. But I absolutely *love* that she was *looking*.

WHAT ARE YOU LOOKING FOR?

We all have times of uncertainty in our lives, but this is what I know to be sure: *anytime* you are feeling unsure or fearful of the future, *anytime* the longing in your soul becomes almost unbearable in the time of waiting, there is *always* a way to walk straight into the security of the arms of our great God. In fact, our expectation—what we are looking for—actually seems to be the breeding ground for the miraculous in our lives.

I love how the poet Robert Robinson wrote about this in the beloved hymn, "Come, Thou Fount of Every Blessing":

> O to grace how great a debtor
> Daily I'm constrained to be!
> Let Thy goodness, like a fetter,
> Bind my wandering heart to Thee.
> Prone to wander, Lord, I feel it,
> Prone to leave the God I love;

Here's my heart, O take and seal it,
Seal it for Thy courts above.[1]

Rather than wandering through his life with no sense of leaning into the unknown, we can hear this hymn writer's prayers cry out for his heart to be tied to the mysteries of God, and his love song of trust rises once more to the God he knows is so very close to him and his circumstances. Rather than settling for a casual commitment, he is looking for more. The power of expectation sets his sight on "Thy courts above."

To find this kind of love in our own lives, we, too, must look for it. God asks us to seek Him and seek Him first—over and above all other loves we may experience in our lives.

The Samaritan woman at the well had experienced many human loves and many man-made relationships, but it was not until she encountered the Lord of love that her needs were truly met and her thirst was truly quenched. Take a look at her familiar story with new eyes.

> Soon a Samaritan woman came to draw water. Jesus said to her, "Give me a drink of water." Surprised, she said, "Why would a Jewish man ask a Samaritan woman for a drink of water?" Jesus replied, "If you only knew who I am and the gift that God wants to give you—you'd ask me for a drink, and I would give to you living water."
>
> The woman replied, "But sir, you don't even have a bucket and this well is very deep. So where do you find this 'living water'? Do you really think that you are greater than our ancestor Jacob who dug this well and drank from it himself, along with his children and livestock?"
>
> Jesus answered, "If you drink from Jacob's well you'll be thirsty again and again, but if anyone drinks the living water I give them, they will never thirst again and will be forever satisfied!

For when you drink the water I give you it becomes a gushing fountain of the Holy Spirit, springing up and flooding you with endless life!"

The woman replied, "Let me drink that water so I'll never be thirsty again and won't have to come back here to draw water."

Jesus said, "Go get your husband and bring him back here."

"But I'm not married," the woman answered.

"That's true," Jesus said, "for you've been married five times and now you're living with a man who is not your husband. You have told the truth."

The woman said, "You must be a prophet! So tell me this: Why do our fathers worship God here on this nearby mountain, but your people teach that Jerusalem is the place where we must worship. Which is right?"

Jesus responded, "Believe me, dear woman, the time has come when you won't worship the Father on a mountain nor in Jerusalem, but in your heart. Your people don't really know the One they worship. We Jews worship out of our experience, for it's from the Jews that salvation is made available. From here on, worshiping the Father will not be a matter of the right place but with the right heart. For God is a Spirit, and he longs to have sincere worshipers who worship and adore him in the realm of the Spirit and in truth."

The woman said, "This is all so confusing, but I do know that the Anointed One is coming—the true Messiah. And when he comes, he will tell us everything we need to know."

Jesus said to her, "You don't have to wait any longer, the Anointed One is here speaking with you—I am the One you're looking for." (John 4:8–26 TPT)

Yes, with Jesus, there is always a "Yes, I have found what I was looking for!" moment to be had. We don't have to wait any longer with fear or sadness to find the fulfillment for the longings of our hearts. We don't have to wait in frustration in times of transition any longer. No, we are called to wait in hope that the newness we've been waiting for is, in fact, within us. Do you realize right now that the Holy Spirit is leading you into all things new?

In worship, we are given the ability and opportunity by the Spirit of God to enter into the courts of God, no matter what season or state we find ourselves in. And as I've already said, as we draw near to God, we find He has been drawing near to us all along, in every season, every moment of our lives.

COME UP HERE!

Revelation 4 presents a picture of how worship opens us up to experiencing our heavenly Father in the fullness of His glory:

> After this I looked, and behold, a door standing open in heaven! And the first voice which I had heard, like the sound of a [war] trumpet speaking with me, said, "Come up here, and I will show you what must take place after these things." At once I was in [special communication with] the Spirit; and behold, a throne stood in heaven, with One seated on the throne. (vv. 1–2 AMP)

"Come up here!" the Spirit called to John.

Can you picture this? A scene in which the Spirit of the Lord was calling John up to enter into heaven's glorious domain, with the majesty of eternal glory spread before him. John was looking, and what he was about to experience would change him forever.

The throne of God, with the King and His kingdom, and all the perfection of heavenly clarity and of God's holiness, was displayed before John in crystal-clear detail. The landscape described in Revelation is pure and holy.

And this is the beauty of worship, expressed here on earth. Worship is our invitation to "come up here," to experience the glory and kindness of the Lord, to simply respond to His request with an open heart. Whenever we pray, as we were instructed in the Lord's Prayer, the words "Thy kingdom come, Thy will be done *on earth*, as it is in heaven," usher us into these moments where we taste and see and experience the all-in-all-ness of the fullness of God—*on this side of heaven!*

What is it that you are looking for and longing to experience today?

His love? His forgiveness?
The weight of His glory?
His kindness and compassion?
To feel His presence and power?
To hear from God?
To enjoy the adventure of knowing God intimately?

True worship gives us the tools we need to push past all the noise going on around us so that we may enter His gates, so that we may "come up here" where our King sits in glory and majesty, where every battle has been won and every tear wiped away.

I love that the woman at the well continued to press into what this new and strange man was saying that was causing her heart to stir. As He spoke, she began to experience the fullness and joy and transformation of salvation. Her soul began to be watered by the rivers of heaven itself. And she soon realized that she'd just found the One she had been searching for all along.

Heaven encountered earth that day. And her "come up here" moment was rewarded with a fountain of living water that would never run dry.

PUSH INTO HIS PRESENCE

Sometimes, my friends, as we open our hearts to follow the call to enter His gates, we may need to "push into His presence" not by striving but by making up our minds that *we will not* leave until God has revealed Himself to us once more. That may sound presumptuous and brash, but consider Jacob, an incredibly blessed and incredibly flawed man who was sick and tired of not living up to his birthright. What did he do? He had the audacity to wrestle with God!

> But Jacob stayed behind by himself, and a man wrestled with him until daybreak. When the man saw that he couldn't get the best of Jacob as they wrestled, he deliberately threw Jacob's hip out of joint. The man said, "Let me go; it's daybreak." Jacob said, "I'm not letting you go 'til you bless me." The man said, "What's your name?" He answered, "Jacob." The man said, "But no longer. Your name is no longer Jacob. From now on it's Israel (God-Wrestler); you've wrestled with God and you've come through." (Genesis 32:24–28 THE MESSAGE)

Can you imagine having so much determination to see Him, to experience Him, that you would spend an entire night wrestling? That even after having a dislocated hip you wouldn't let go?

Sometimes, my friend, that is what it takes. There have been many moments over the years in leading worship where the atmosphere was just *so* heavy. I sensed such disappointment in the room or it was obvious that people were distracted. I don't have the strength to wrestle an angel all night, but as those who know and love me will agree, I do have some fight in me. In such moments of discouragement or lethargy, I knew that I had to push. Call it a wildness of determination in my spirit, but I was determined that *we were going to worship*!

Okay, in the end, I know I cannot make people worship. But I also know that I can lead and do my very best to be resolute in following the Holy Spirit as He leads. I know that I can ignore the enemy when he tries to whisper to me, "This is fake! This is too hard. Who do you think you are that you can lead people to worship?"

It can feel disheartening to see so many people—even in the church—who are finding the holes in their souls deepening and widening; they are grasping at straws to fill the void. But even as the noise of the world proclaiming that we don't need God anymore gets louder and louder, it's essential to remember that we are to declare God's kingdom as we gather together and worship Jesus. The church is alive and well. The kingdom of God *is* advancing. The golden thread has not been broken.

God's kingdom is immovable and unshakable. It is vital to not only remember this reality but to also celebrate it. When we worship—even if we have to *push* into worship—we do not allow the kingdoms of this world to small us down or drown us out. On the other side of your obedience is God's magnificent pleasure, His voice and His heart longing to be heard above the noise of the storms that can rage and the winds that can howl like fear around the recesses of your soul.

FAITH IS THE KEY

At these times, this is where faith is simply that: faith. Being sure of what you do not see, by grace, through faith. It's not fake. Fake cannot produce the miraculous, and fake cannot shake a mountain and throw it into the sea. Fake cannot heal a broken heart, and fake could never have rescued humanity from an eternity spent in separation from God. Oh, but faith! Faith will draw us into His presence!

Without faith, it is impossible to please God, but *with* faith, even just the tiniest bit, all things become possible! Worship—in spirit and in truth—by *faith!*—will lead you by the hand into heaven's throne room: from fear to love, from impossible to possible!

There is nothing like His presence.

LORD, I AM COMING!

What is the goal of our worship anyway? It should always be to see Jesus and to experience His presence.

What is the outcome of our truthful worship? We are changed by His presence, and we then take His presence into the world.

When I first started leading worship, it was such an overwhelmingly breathtaking time, because there was no pull on me other than the "come up here" of worship. I was able to seek Him first above all others, and I was rewarded by the glory of His sweet presence.

There is always such freedom when we discover as a church and as a worship team the wonder, power, and freedom that is always available in God's presence. The simplicity of worship has sometimes been challenged, misguided, battered, and bruised along the way, but the psalmist taught us how to respond. When God tells us that there is more, when He asks us to come up and be with Him in His presence, follow these instructions of the great hymn writer of the Psalms:

> My heart has heard you say, "Come and talk with me." And my heart responds, "Lord, I am coming." (Psalm 27:8 NLT)

"Lord, I am coming!" Cry that along with the psalmist and all others who desire to heed His call to their hearts to come and be with Him, to seek Him first.

I sense that one of the enemy's great weapons across the earth today is *distraction*. We all can be distracted by so many things: our phones, the constant pull on our time to be busier, to do more and accomplish more each day. And yet when we hunger for Him and dive into the depths of God's Word and His love for us, oh, there is so much that we discover in His presence: so much prophecy, so much creativity, so many weapons that cannot be released without time spent in His presence.

Seek Jesus first. Make time with Him your priority. You are His priority—so make Him yours!

God Himself desired John to come up higher. And God Himself called John into a deeper dimension of the Spirit. What I love the most about this is that John simply said yes to the Lord's invitation. John's beautiful response, found in Revelation 22:8–9, took place near the end of this revelatory moment: He simply fell to his knees in worship. At first, the angel who was speaking to him said, "John, don't worship me. Worship Jesus!"

But John's posture of reverence and humility shone through this moment. And as he was called up, his posture in a life filled with worship drew him back to his knees.

God has extended this invitation to "come up" to all of us, offering us all the benefits of His indescribable love in our lives. So lift up your head and come into His presence, as Psalm 24:7–10 (TPT) directs us to do:

> So wake up, you living gateways!
> Lift up your heads, you ageless doors of destiny!
> Welcome the King of Glory,
> for he is about to come through you.
> You ask, "Who is this Glory-King?"
> The Lord, armed and ready for battle,
> the Mighty One, invincible in every way!
> So wake up, you living gateways, and rejoice!
> Fling wide, you ageless doors of destiny!

Here he comes; the King of Glory is ready to come in.
You ask, "Who is this King of Glory?"
He is the Lord of Victory, armed and ready for battle,
the Mighty One, the invincible commander of heaven's hosts!
Yes, he is the King of Glory!

FREE BEFORE THE LORD

In the Old Testament, David modeled something in his posture of worship that was profound in an age when everyone worshipped idols. With so much opposition around him, David still found a way to push through the noise of the day to pursue the worship of God, in both the tough seasons and the seasons of extreme blessing. We can see that the posture of David's heart was one of humility, even after he made the greatest mistakes of his life. Whatever life threw at David, he always came back to repentance, continually bringing his life back into worship of God, his King. David continually humbled himself and maintained a "come up here" response to God's heart for him.

David was free before the Lord, undignified but wholehearted. I think that's the key. If we worry about what others think, or get caught in our performance, a spiral downward is inevitable.

We will always become like what we worship. If we worship money, we will become greedy. If we worship pleasure and comfort, we will become hedonistic. If we worship God, if we seek first His kingdom, if our eyes are fixed on Jesus, the Author and Perfecter of our faith (Hebrews 12:2), we will grow in godliness, we will become Christlike.

The golden thread of God's redemptive power and love has been present for us before the foundation of the earth. Even if we stray, the golden thread will pull us back to the arms of our heavenly Father. But when we seek Him first, the power and protection and guidance and spiritual nourishment become so much more profound in our lives.

The more time you spend seeking Him first in everything, and in every decision of life, the more you will become like Him. When you put yourself completely into the hands of God and let Him shape your heart and heal your emotions and set the direction of your life—oh my, you will never find anything else as beautiful to focus on; you will never want to let go of the golden thread of His presence in your life.

3

WHAT AN ADVENTURE!

*Faith never knows where one is being led, but
it knows and loves the One who is leading.*
—OSWALD CHAMBERS, *MY UTMOST FOR HIS HIGHEST*

IT WAS A DAY LIKE ANY OTHER. TWO OF OUR DAUGHTERS WERE still in school, so the day started with getting everyone fed and ready for the day, making lunches and checking assignments, hitting the gym, doing a little bit of writing, and planning dinner. (I love to cook!) We were living in the home we had designed and built ourselves, the house we thought would be our forever home. Amy, our eldest daughter, was now married to Andrew, so we had even built a little "imagination garden" in preparation for the day when we had grandchildren! (Talk about pressure for our kids to have kids of their own!)

We had been part of a dynamic church family for twenty-seven years, so we were surrounded by lifelong, treasured relationships. We had a history in the ministry there that was life-shaping and life-changing. Our daughters had attended one school and one church their entire lives. Our youngest daughter had only lived in one house.

From the outside it might have seemed an idyllic situation, and mostly, from the inside, it was. But frustration had started to bubble up inside of me, gently at first but then growing in force, nagging at my heart. And the crazy thing was, there was nothing I could pinpoint that warranted this kind of frustration. There were the normal things, you know, always wanting to improve some area of my life, getting frustrated when things weren't quite working the way I thought they should. But the typical beauty of seasons of frustration is that they do have a way of calling your knees to the carpet, nudging you to lay hold of God in ways you might not otherwise do when all is well in your world. I could sense the Holy Spirit speaking to my heart during this time, asking me to let go of some things that had grown too important to me. My soul was in a quandary, and I felt as if I was about to leap out of a plane with no safe landing space available.

It wasn't just me. Mark was going through a similar experience. And so, my husband, who has always been an early riser, with a cup of coffee in one hand and his Bible in the other, started to get even more intentional during his morning prayers. And I mean *really* intentional. I could feel the shift taking place in our home, and I could see it in his eyes. It seemed like he was wrestling with God over something. He had been a part of building some really wonderful ministries in the past, and now he was in the middle of building an incredible media company; the hand of God was on it, but we knew a shift was coming. I watched him and prayed for him as he daily went to his threshing floor to seek the Lord.

We found ourselves in a long season of transition. After I decided to resign from working full-time at the church and go back to just volunteer activities, my life started to take on a new rhythm. It was a rhythm that, I have to say, I was finding very difficult adjusting to, with fewer appointments and more time on my hands just to *be*. But I knew beyond a shadow of a doubt that this was what God was calling me to do, and so I was learning to yield to His season of change in my life. I just continued to lean into my sacred friendship with God, as He taught me more and more about His love for me and how it stayed true regardless of what work I did for Him. We'll chat more about that in a bit.

In the meantime, during this time of life the winds of change were blowing gently in our world and God's kindness continued to draw us closer to His heart. We had to allow the frustration we were experiencing in our circumstances to keep drawing us to Him. It's such a funny thing to feel like you have achieved everything in your life you've ever deemed important—and yet you somehow sense, *there's got to be more*. Were we being ridiculous? Were we being overly selfish? Shouldn't we just "settle down"?

Mark and I prayed and chatted with our pastor and close friends about how we were sensing a change on the horizon and how we had *little* idea what our restless feelings were all about. After all this, imagine my surprise when one morning, coffee in hand, Mark simply asked, "Would you like to have another adventure?"

A NEW THING

An adventure? Sure. Who doesn't like an adventure?

Now, I am not a great one for camping. I do, however, love to go fishing, and so I thought maybe Mark meant that there would be some fly fishing in my near future. (Wishful thinking?) I never in a million years suspected the next words that came out of his mouth: "I think that maybe God is asking us to lead a church."

Are you . . .

The only thing we'd ever said to each other about leading a church was that it was always such a *great honor* to serve our church leaders—and we'd definitely served some of the best! We'd always said that we'd never want to lead a church, but that we'd both rather lift up the arms of others who were called to that realm of leadership. So, who was this man who was standing in front of me, suggesting this crazy idea? Oh, that's right, he's the man I married—the man who had been wrestling with God for some time over an idea the Holy Spirit had whispered to him a while ago, yet an idea he could not truly believe himself!

Truth be told, my emotions were everywhere after I heard his words. My loyalties were confused, and I could hardly think straight. Could this possibly be God? But over time, whenever I allowed myself to be still during those tumultuous days, it seemed like a calming wave of steadfast peace undergirded my thoughts, thoughts that were certainly all over the place! My emotions were not to be trusted during those days.

I remember my dad always telling us kids never to make life-changing decisions if your emotions were out of control, and based on those wise words of advice, Mark and I stayed put and continued to worship and pray and to talk and dream. We kept our routines as normal as possible for the sake of our kids and the people we loved, and we worked hard not to allow this coming season of transition to dull our senses and close our hearts. Long transitions, or long seasons of our hearts being stretched, tend to cause more damage than we anticipate.

Slowly but surely, however, I started to embrace the change in which Mark had already quietly and patiently immersed himself. I would never want to be the one who was dragging the chain against

God's will. (Hmmm, long story I could digress into here, but in our first big change as a married couple, it was yours truly who was *extremely slow* to the party!)

The golden thread of God's love for me was leading me in a new direction, but I was having a hard time believing this could be true. As my heart slowly grew warmer and warmer to the idea, the words of the prophet Isaiah beckoned me:

> Do not remember the former things, nor consider the things of old. Behold, I will do a new thing, now it shall spring forth; shall you not know it? (Isaiah 43:18–19 NKJV)

In this passage, the Lord Himself is asking the question: "Do you want to open yourself to My new thing?" These words echo down through the span of time, and He asks the same question of our generation of believers today.

Whenever these words are spoken—"the *new* thing"—I know that for me it fuels an excitement in my spirit, maybe even a nervous excitement. I think about all the things I need to walk away from, things I need to let go of. But I've said it many times before, it's hard to take hold of the new when you are holding on too tightly to the old. I felt the tug of God's golden thread of purpose starting to pull me closer toward Him so that I could hear His voice. At first, God gently whispered to me, but as the clarity of the "new thing" started to take shape, His voice grew louder and louder. There was no way I could miss Him calling to us for a new adventure.

In this scripture, the word *new* actually means "unprecedented in its wonderful character" (look back at Isaiah 42:9). So when we are considering something from God to us that is *brand-new*, we are not referring to just an upgrade or a tidy up. This is a complete overhaul.

The Bible is full of examples of God doing *brand-new* things!

God calls us a *new* creation.
He declares a *new* heaven and a *new* earth.
He says to sing *new* songs.

He is a God who delights in taking old things—old memories, old lives, old shame—and making them new.

For here's what I'm going to do: I'm going to take you out of these countries, gather you from all over, and bring you back to your own land. I'll pour pure water over you and scrub you clean. I'll give you a new heart, put a new spirit in you. I'll remove the stone heart from your body and replace it with a heart that's God-willed, not self-willed. I'll put my Spirit in you and make it possible for you to do what I tell you and live by my commands. You'll once again live in the land I gave your ancestors. You'll be my people! I'll be your God! (Ezekiel 36:26–28 THE MESSAGE)

GOD IS IN THE "NOW"

Often, we think that we want the new, but we really don't want the process of pain that change may require in order to bring the new to pass.

Trust is a verb. It includes leaning on the character of Christ, especially when you cannot see what is in front of you. It is letting go of control so that you can trust God with the process. It is a daily walk, the putting of one foot in front of the other as you steward those things you know and as you do your best with the things you don't know.

So, longer story short, Mark and I moved with our family up to the Central Coast of Australia and took on a church. Was it hard at times? Certainly. Has it always been a blessing? Undoubtedly. The last almost ten years of my life, since saying yes to God's new adventure, have been filled with His teaching me about His un-relenting love for me. And let me encourage you, the more you focus on His love, the more you will willingly give up wanting to keep control, as His plans for our lives are *far* greater than our own!

The God who is in your past is the same God who is in your future, and He is the very same God of your *now*—your *today*. Isaiah finished his powerful prophetic picture in Isaiah 43:18–19 with the following line: "Now it shall spring forth."

Just because you don't see the "new" God has in store for you, doesn't mean it hasn't started! This is just part of learning to walk by faith.

The Hebrew word *spring* is the very same word used for "sprout." I think the trouble most of us have with the word *now* here is that we believe surely this means we will see something fully developed now—as in, *right now*. We live in a society filled with instant gratification, where our patience is tested if we must wait thirty seconds for the microwave. We want things now! So much so that if you look at the rate our world continues to accumulate debt, you will see a definite lack of wisdom that much of the Western world applies generously to having things *right now*. The art of championing delayed gratification is almost lost, which will only continue to have a negative impact on society into the future.

Isaiah is reminding us that God's promises are usually a part of a process, part of a greater story and you may not see it now, but you must learn to trust Him to bring them to pass. Martin Luther King Jr. put it powerfully and succinctly when he said, "Faith is taking the first step, even when you don't see the whole staircase."

Our family owns a beautiful garden center on the Central Coast. It's interesting to see the place in winter, when there are not as many blooms about. Our beautiful roses get shy and stop showing off their perfect colors. But there is still a beauty to be seen in the winter buds and even the plants that look like twigs that the untrained eye might think are dead and ready for the compost heap.

But if you walk around these plants with trained horticulturalists, you will begin to feel their expectation—for they *know* what is about to spring forth, as time does what only time can do. Solomon understood this and expressed it with a poetic beauty:

> For behold, the winter is past;
>   the rain is over and gone.
> The flowers appear on the earth,
>   the time of singing has come,
> and the voice of the turtledove
>   is heard in our land.
> The fig tree ripens its figs,
>   and the vines are in blossom;
>   they give forth fragrance.
> Arise, my love, my beautiful one,
>   and come away.
>
> (Song of Solomon 2:11–13 esv)

As Pastor Jack Hayford said,

What the Lord wants us to understand when He says He's going to do a new thing is that it is in process already. You can't see it yet, but it's set in motion; just like after a long, cold winter, there's a change going on inside the Earth underground, preparing to bring the approach of spring. Beyond what has perhaps been the cold, bitter winter of your soul—or the drought of a long dry spell—the Lord says He's set in motion that which will bring about deliverance unto a time of growth, development, refreshing, and fruitfulness. When God's "new thing" sprouts in you, it will be with the fragrance and beauty of the springtime of His purpose in you.[1]

I am always amazed when I see blocks of concrete, so solid and seemingly impenetrable, uprooted and cracked by something that actually started its life as a mere sprout! In the same way, God's new thing in your life will break through *any* barrier it needs to. Our job is to trust and to be diligent and confident during the season of our stretching and testing.

From a prison cell, Paul wrote to you and me words of encouragement and confidence:

> Being confident of this very thing, that He who has begun a good work in you will complete it until the day of Jesus Christ. (Philippians 1:6 NKJV)

David wrote that faith in God looks like this: "Be still, and know that I am God" (Psalm 46:10 NIV).

A JOURNEY OF TRUST

What a journey it has been thus far. I am so grateful to my husband, who has been so brave when I have been timid. And I am so grateful to a God who works with timid people like me to bring about a new thing in the earth.

In your own life, believe that He has begun the good work, that the sprout has begun to take root.

By using the word *know*, Isaiah shed additional understanding on God's new work in our lives:

> Do not remember the former things, nor consider the things of old. Behold, I will do a new thing, now it shall spring forth; shall you not know it? (Isaiah 43:18–19 NKJV)

The word *know* in the Hebrew language implies far more than head knowledge, but rather likens *knowing* with the total giving of yourself, like watching a child jump wildly into the arms of a parent with *no* fear because she just *knows* her parent will catch her. The Lord is saying, "I'm going to do a new thing in your life. But for you to truly know it will require an even greater intimacy with Me, so that you can hear Me speak, watch Me work, learn to trust completely that My heart is for you, and know that My kingdom is at work in you."

The context of this Scripture is God's delivering the children of Israel from slavery in Egypt. Even after the miracle of escaping from the prison of persecution and isolation in another land, and just when they thought they were finally free, they faced yet another "small problem." The Red Sea blocked them from their destination, and Pharaoh's armies were relentlessly pursuing them. But thank God that Moses knew His voice and followed His commands. The sea drowned those who would have destroyed them. God turned the world upside down once more for the good of His people.

Surprisingly, after God reminds us of the mighty new thing that He did for the children of Israel at the Red Sea, He tells us: "Do not remember the former things, nor consider the things of old" (v. 18).

Does that make sense? Aren't we to remember to remember what God has done for us?

We are never to forget God's faithfulness to us. And no question, our God of miracles can do the same miracles again and again. But in telling us to forget and let go, He is asking us to not confine Him to what He's already done. The miracle at the Red Sea was beyond anyone's ability to comprehend not only in that day but even today; yet there will always be new things that God wants to do for us, things that are so far beyond anything we could ever dream, invent, ask, or imagine! Ephesians 3:20 tells us that God is able to do "exceedingly abundantly above all that we ask or think, according to the power that works in us" (NKJV).

If Mark and I had confined God to the amazing things He had

already done in our lives, we would still be in Sydney and have missed the new thing He wanted to do in us up the coast.

I can guarantee that when we say yes to following Jesus, we will never know all the details about the "new thing" that God is up to in our lives. Even so, our hearts can remain at peace, knowing that He is going to lead us and prepare us for all that lies ahead. Trust is developed over time, and the more you understand God's heart for you and how He longs to bless your life, the more you will learn to trust Him and take Him at His Word.

Transition is always hard. But just like what happened when I first said yes to Jesus' love, He in turn said, "Come, follow Me." When He calls you, truly the safest place you could ever be is hidden in Him, as your yes leads you to the fulfilment of His amazing plans for your life!

GOD IS NOT LIMITED

Paul was never one to say no to the new. Once God got hold of Paul's heart on the road to Damascus, his life was a series of new things: a new faith, a new name, a new mission, a new continent—whatever God asked Paul to do, wherever God asked Paul to go, his answer was always yes.

Consider ways Paul embraced the "new":

So if you're serious about living this new resurrection life with Christ, act like it. Pursue the things over which Christ presides. Don't shuffle along, eyes to the ground, absorbed with the things right in front of you. Look up, and be alert to what is going on around Christ—that's where the action is. See things from his perspective.

Your old life is dead. Your new life, which is your real life— even though invisible to spectators—is with Christ in God. He is your life. When Christ (your real life, remember) shows up again on this earth, you'll show up, too—the real you, the glorious you. Meanwhile, be content with obscurity, like Christ. . . .

So, chosen by God for this new life of love, dress in the wardrobe God picked out for you: compassion, kindness, humility, quiet strength, discipline. Be even-tempered, content with second place, quick to forgive an offense. Forgive as quickly and completely as the Master forgave you. And regardless of what else you put on, wear love. It's your basic, all-purpose garment. Never be without it. (Colossians 3:1–4, 12–14 THE MESSAGE)

What is it you are believing God for?
Where is God leading you?
What fears are holding you back?
Are you ready for the *new* in your life?
Will you be still and *know*?
Are you willing to say yes?

Let's believe God together that if you sense you are on the edge of something new, you will be brave enough to take the leap into God's great goodness. "A man's mind plans his way [as he journeys through life], but the LORD directs his steps *and* establishes them" (Proverbs 16:9 AMP).

Did you catch that? God will steer you in the right direction. God will secure your steps.

For Mark and me and our family, once we fully said yes and took the leap, in many ways the new was easier than I imagined it could be. Apart from missing lots of my friends in my day to day, the rest has been quite miraculous on so many levels. Watching God do in our hearts what only He could do and putting our roots down in a new area has been overwhelming, but at the same time it feels like a perfect fit. It's been an adventure of faith!

Maybe you've made some wrong turns in the past that are

blocking you from moving forward and saying yes to the new thing God wants to do in your life. We are gently reminded to forget what is behind, and to reach toward all that is ahead (Philippians 3:13). Don't let the hurts, disappointments, and regrets from the past cripple your present or define your future.

It's exciting to see those things that start as a simple thought—a momentary, fleeting thought—actually come to life. That's how songs are birthed. Ideas for songs, melodies, sounds, chords, and lyrics are always floating around in my heart and in my head—sometimes a scary place to live! Sometimes I have one foot in heaven and the other here on earth—absolutely no use to anyone at all in a practical sense.

And then, hours or weeks or months later, I'll be singing that very song over a congregation—and even more astonishing, they'll be singing it back to me. I think about the power of bringing to the fore that which is in my heart. But it doesn't go from my heart to my hands by wishing it there. It comes by sticking with the idea, working diligently, listening and learning, disciplining myself to finish writing the song, and then living with the conviction that the Spirit of the Lord has put that song into my heart and my life for a very real purpose. Sometimes that purpose is just for me and Him.

God is always multiplying and adding to our dreams, and His purpose is more clearly unveiled as you and I pursue the process and begin to walk it out.

God is not limited by all the things which, at the moment, you feel are your limitations. He has something for you that will perfectly fit your gifts, your talents, and your calling. Embrace your vision with a passion for God and trust in His ability to do the impossible. Why don't you start today? Write it down, talk it out, pray about what you are sensing, and anchor it in your heart. God delights in seeing His dreams for our lives transition from one generation to the next. It's time to take back the territory that has been stolen by the enemy and allow the dreams of the Lord to be perpetuated into the future generations.

You see, the golden thread of God's love for us didn't just begin before the foundations of the world—His golden thread will outlive our mortal bodies.

King David put God at the center of all that he did. He had a vision for building a temple that would glorify God—a temple that would far exceed his own palace. He gathered the materials to build the temple, but it was his son Solomon who completed the dream.

What could you see taking place in your life if you had no limitations? Don't be afraid to dream beyond your own capabilities. Who says you can't do everything that is in your heart to do! Our longings to serve Jesus are the best motivation to fuel our dreams.

Are you ready for an adventure? Take hold of the golden thread of God's presence to discover the new thing He has planned for you!

4

SEND ME!

Lord, whatever you want, wherever you want it,
and whenever you want it, that's what I want.
—RICHARD BAXTER

THE FIRST TIME WE SEE THE WORD *WORSHIP* MENTIONED IN SCRIPTURE is in Genesis 22, which tells the dramatic story of Abraham and his beloved son Isaac: "Some time later God tested Abraham. He said to him, 'Abraham!' 'Here I am,' he replied" (v. 1 NIV).

Our English definition of the word *worship* gives no hint as to what our wholehearted response to God must be. "Here I am," was Abraham's response. The Hebrew word used for this statement is *hineni*, meaning, "Whatever it is you ask of me, Lord, *before* You even ask, my answer is yes!" That is the response of a heart of worship!

Then God said, "Take your son, your only son, whom you

love—Isaac—and go to the region of Moriah. Sacrifice him there as a burnt offering on a mountain I will show you" (v. 2 NIV).

Oh, my. Could any command strike more anguish and terror in the heart of a parent? What did Abraham, a man who had longed so long for a son, do?

> Early the next morning Abraham got up and loaded his donkey. He took with him two of his servants and his son Isaac. When he had cut enough wood for the burnt offering, he set out for the place God had told him about. . . .
>
> When they reached the place God had told him about, Abraham built an altar there and arranged the wood on it. He bound his son Isaac and laid him on the altar, on top of the wood. Then he reached out his hand and took the knife to slay his son. (v. 3, 9–10 NIV)

We know what happened next. With a rush of great relief to Abraham—and to those of us reading this passage—God sent a ram for the sacrifice, sparing Abraham's son from death. Did Abraham know how this would turn out? I don't think so, but he was prophetic when he answered Isaac's question about where the sacrifice was by saying, "God will provide a sheep for the burnt offering, my son" (v. 8 NLT).

The Lord's response to Abraham's act of faith is incredible:

> The angel of the LORD called to Abraham from heaven a second time and said, "I swear by myself, declares the LORD, that because you have done this and have not withheld your son, your only son, I will surely bless you and make your descendants as numerous as the stars in the sky and as the sand on the seashore. Your descendants will take possession of the cities of their enemies, and through your offspring all nations on earth will be blessed, because you have obeyed me." (vv. 15–18 NIV)

YOU WITHHELD NOTHING

Because you have withheld nothing from me, in blessing I will bless you.

I am always challenged by this test of faith. Even the fact that Abraham rose *early* in the morning in obedience to God's voice speaks to me. I would love to say, "Oh, of course, every time God speaks, I respond quickly!" But in this case, I cannot even fathom the process and the wholehearted *yes* that emerged from this godly leader.

Notice that when Abraham was about to bring this most expensive of offerings, his son, in worship, there was no mention of music or song. Instead, at the center of this picture, there was an altar—and the treasure of someone's heart about to be laid on it. The story of Abraham and Isaac teaches us that worship is not so much what we do with our lips but, rather, what we do with our lives. Like the miracle ram in the thicket, when we are seeking God and His purposes, we will find that He has been making a way for us all along. The indescribable fullness of His nearness, His presence—the golden thread he has woven into our lives—is with us always. No wonder we call Jesus the great Emmanuel.

We are to offer our lives as a living sacrifice:

> Therefore, I urge you, brothers and sisters, in view of God's mercy, to offer your bodies as a living sacrifice, holy and pleasing to God—this is your true and proper worship. Do not conform to the pattern of this world, but be transformed by the renewing of your mind. Then you will be able to test and approve what God's will is—his good, pleasing and perfect will. (Romans 12:1–2 NIV)

Woven throughout the miracle of worship, I believe that as the church (every single one of us who knows Jesus across the entire world), we are all being called by the Holy Spirit into this posture of obedience: hands upward and open, ready for whatever is asked of us, and declaring with all our hearts: "Here I am, Lord, send me," just as the prophet Isaiah, a teenager at the time, declared after seeing the glory of the Lord while in worship (Isaiah 6:1–8 NLT). We respond this way, not out of guilt or gritty determination, but as our worshipful response to the beauty of His presence and the call to His purposes.

DON'T LOSE YOUR SONG

But have we lost sight of the golden thread? Have we lost our sense of wonder and worship in the presence of God? We live in a world that is full of busyness and noise, affluence and poverty, crazy political shifts, war and violence, and dire suffering and pain. At times it can feel like parts of the church across the earth are starting to retreat, to sit down and just become part of the landscape, perhaps overwhelmed with the magnitude of her mission.

In the last Australian census, it was noted that the majority in our country felt the church in general has become unimportant, an unattractive option for those wanting some peace for their souls. And then there is the sad fact of Christians blurring the line between faith and disbelief and reducing God's kingdom to simply a lifestyle choice. And so, instead of standing our ground, taking our place in this world, singing our songs, stepping into our part of God's glorious redemption plan, we step back. We give in to the lullaby of comfort which gently sings us to sleep. I've heard it said that every time the church loses its voice, the world loses its conscience. How true!

One of the saddest verses in all of Scripture was penned by Solomon: "The elders are gone from the city gate; the young men have stopped their music" (Lamentations 5:14 NIV).

When Moses faced this issue, wondering if he was moving forward without God showing him the way, he made a powerful stance, an intentional statement about the absolute necessity of God's presence always being front and center in his life. What Moses ultimately said to the Lord was this: "If Your presence does not come with us, then we are not going anywhere!"

There is an enemy at work on the earth. He works in ways he always has, as an angel of light or a roaring lion. "Your enemy, the devil, roams around incessantly, like a roaring lion looking for its prey to devour" (1 Peter 5:8 TPT). However he attacks us, his purpose has never changed. He comes at us to kill, steal, and destroy. We should never forget Paul's warning about the enemy: "For our struggle is not against flesh and blood, but against the rulers, against the authorities, against the powers of this dark world and against the spiritual forces of evil in the heavenly realms" (Ephesians 6:12 NIV).

One of the ways evil will try to destroy your influence is to convince you to make *silence* your stance. Keeping you quiet about your faith will steal your joy, your song, and your authority. Kingdom culture is created through presence and language. And when kingdom culture is silenced, this brings confusion, distrust, and exclusivity. I am not talking about our need for quiet, for peace in our souls. I am addressing when it is our time to speak, to stand and declare for God. We lose so much in those moments when we know we should speak up but we stay silent.

Adam lost his authority as he stayed silent. Esther had to learn to speak up for the sake of her people and saved her people from devastation. She changed the mind of a king.

How often have we lost our God-given dominion over our world due to our silence, choosing comfort over calling, choosing nice and tidy expressions of service rather than lives laid down for the sake of Christ?

I had a season in my life when even in the midst of doing ministry, even though through my body and my voice I was physically doing my best, my heart had become disconnected and my soul had wearied, just trying to cope with the busyness of my days.

Not a good place to be. And it was worse because I couldn't seem to find my way to speak up on what was happening with me. I couldn't find my footing and by remaining silent, I wasn't receiving the help and wisdom I needed.

I'm not blaming anyone else. It was my own fault. I had buried my voice in busyness so I could not speak what was on my heart and needed to be said. Sometimes the comfort of doing what is known is much more appealing than delving into the unknown. But the golden thread of God's kindness and grace reached into my being once more. He met me where I needed Him most—this is who He is. When I stopped to listen, I was reminded that the Lord doesn't need our busyness and He is not impressed with how many items are listed on our schedules.

No, God wants our presence in His presence, so that we will know His heart and hear Him speak as we live out the love of Christ in the world around us.

LIVE YOUR LIFE ON PURPOSE

Dear friend, as we choose again to live life on purpose, for His purpose, as we live life as an offering of worship unto Jesus, we pull heaven close. We stand in the weight of God's eternal worth, and we establish yet again where our greatest priorities lie. I wrote a book called *Worship Changes Everything*, and I believe with all my heart that worship does change everything. As I stop to truly see and hear from God, there is a change that occurs in me as the Holy Spirit draws me close.

Abraham's response to God's command on the mountain was not a choice born out of a spur-of-the-moment feeling. Abraham's entire life was lived as one who loved God and who knew God loved him. His response was born out of the way he had already decided to live his life in faith and obedience.

Is it any wonder he had such an acute sense of purpose in his life? After all, he had staked his life, his family's life, and the lives of his people on God's Word to him: "I will make you into a great nation. I will bless you and make you famous, and you will be a blessing to others" (Genesis 12:2 NLT). He was a blessed blesser. God's song entered his life, and Abraham sang the song all his days.

A worshipful life does not need all the circumstances of our lives to be perfect. When our eyes are on Jesus, we will worship *despite* some circumstances, *within* some circumstances, but always in *all* circumstances.

> At the bottom of your very worst day, worship.
> At the height of your best day, worship.
> Are you disappointed? Then worship.
> Feeling rejected? Worship.

Make a decision that you *are* a worshipper of the Almighty. Worship is not a function of simply our emotions. Our emotions are important, but it's a decision of our will, enabled by the Spirit, and expressed in many ways.

If you continually allow your emotions to be in the driver's seat, then eventually your worship will fail. If you take the experience of worship and make it all about you—all about your opportunities, your feelings, and your ways—and you don't allow the Spirit of God to transform you from the inside out, then you will miss the greatness of His glory at work in your life. *But* by His grace, if you allow a life of leaning into worship to take your heart on the Jesus journey again and again; to behold the beauty, majesty, grace, and person of the Lord; you will continually be surprised at all you discover in Him.

More than all our doing and achievements, God's presence in our lives is our defining feature—not skills or talents, though these bring Him much glory; no status or title, though He can use these things to bring influence and change. There is nothing like the unmistakable greatness of God drawing near to our unmistakable humanness. This perfect and consistent, timeless and eternal presence of God has taken my life and pulled me from the ashes and given me *so* much more than I ever dreamed possible. There are many times when I simply fall to my knees and thank Him for His great mercy on my complex life, at times wishing I had done some things differently, and yet experiencing the gentle and loving ways the Holy Spirit loves me back to seeing who I am in Him.

I am humbled when I think of the times God spoke to Abraham and Moses and Joshua and David and His prophets, how Jesus drew near to an outcast woman at a well, how God spoke to a young virgin through an angel, how He spoke and created the earth and the planets and every living thing above and under the earth through His word. And yet, He still longs to dwell in me and you, and lead us in the way that only He can.

Say to Him today: "Here I am, Lord, send me!"

What are you waiting for? As you learn to trust God with the entirety of your life, and as you allow His love to permeate and transform every fiber of your being, I guarantee you will be surprised at how the Holy Spirit will lead you and speak to you every step of the way as you walk into His great plan for your life.

> The lovers of God who chase after righteousness will find all their dreams come true: an abundant life drenched with favor and a fountain that overflows with satisfaction.
>
> A warrior filled with wisdom ascends into the high place and releases regional breakthrough, bringing down the strongholds of the mighty. (Proverbs 21:21–22 TPT)

I believe the purpose behind our worship is even greater than we have ever imagined. Maybe, just maybe, the God of all of heaven and earth is reminding us, as we stand to behold Him, that we are made in His image—that we are His image-bearers, and our identity is secure.

As worship and surrender begin and as Jesus reminds us who we are in Him, the revelation of His purposes will result in our godly exterior behavior—starting with expressions of love and devotion that affect every single part of our existence. The revolution of our worship and service is turning our world right side up. We don't need to be striving, just loving, living out our daily *hineni*, "here I am," walking in the power of the miraculous every single day of our lives.

We were made to love and include others around us.

We were made for purpose, on purpose.

We were made to bring joy and to release more of heaven's atmosphere into this earth.

We were made to announce and declare the sovereignty and lordship of King Jesus.

We were made to be the hands and feet of Jesus in this world. And the more we know Him—truly know Him—the more like Him we will become.

We were made to walk in authority.

We were made to gather the outcast ones, to love the unlovable, to stand in the gap, to speak up for those who have no voice of their own.

We were made for *love*! And our God of purpose has designed for us to be changed in His presence and to then take His presence into our world.

God comes here to dwell where His people worship. He inhabits our praises, and wherever that happens, all the weight of His glory, His lordship, and His dominion is present among us.

Lord, let Your kingdom come! We are the habitation for His presence.

I BREATHE TO SERVE

When I first became a Christian, amazingly and very naturally, my response to the great love of God that was now alive in my heart was the *need* to worship. It was a strong need to serve, since I had been made new, and I can literally say that now everything within me was becoming new. I suddenly had new eyes and new ears—and now I understand that this was because God had given me a new heart: "I will give you a new heart and put a new spirit in you; I will remove from you your heart of stone and give you a heart of flesh" (Ezekiel 36:26 NIV).

I still remember how confusing this season of my life really was, as I didn't know anything about worship or the calling of God. I just knew that music for music's sake was no longer the right fit for me. I had a purpose greater than myself. I had been blessed and I had to bless others. It was almost as if I had to serve if I was to breathe.

And so there I was, now joined in spirit to the One who deserved all glory and dominion forever, and by God's grace, my life had finally become a part of giving Him all that glory (Revelation 1:5–6). I was learning how to live my life in worship of the One who loved us and washed us from our sins in His own blood, the One who has made us kings and priests to His God and Father. And as I did this, something like wildfire rose up in me and started to take hold of me to bring about my life's purpose.

Truthful worship will not be politely applauded or ignored. The atmosphere around you will shift and shake as it morphs to the sound of heaven in your heart, releasing His glory in your life and releasing heaven on earth. Greater than man's opinion of you is the lordship of Christ over you. Greater than any personal failures or disappointments you may have encountered is your obedient response to the lordship of Christ in you. By grace we say again and again, "Here I am, Lord, send me!"

5

STRENGTH IN
WEAKNESS

What God expects us to attempt, He
also enables us to achieve.
—STEPHEN OLFORD, *THE GRACE OF GIVING*

I LOVE BEING AROUND PEOPLE WHO LIVE OUT THEIR LIVES WITH hope and service as their "default position." This is one of the reasons I love being a part of a church family, filled with so many everyday people who are living out their days to lift the lives of others. And I've always been inspired by people who have found glorious inner strength during the hardest of times. When I read about people such as Corrie ten Boom or Nelson Mandela, the loudest part of their stories to me is their attitudes toward their circumstances. They made daily, and I am sure hourly, decisions to pursue forgiveness, to honor, to keep serving others, and to maintain a sweet spirit no matter what happened around them. This, to me, is the secret of the influence they wielded in the world.

But where does such inner strength come from?

Corrie ten Boom once said: "Trying to do the Lord's work in your own strength is the most confusing, exhausting, and tedious of all work. But when you are filled with the Holy Spirit, then the ministry of Jesus just flows out of you."[1]

She is echoing the principle that Solomon shared with us in God's Word: "A generous person will prosper; whoever refreshes others will be refreshed" (Proverbs 11:25 NIV).

One young Australian man, Nick Vujicic, is a modern-day miracle man. He was born with Tetra-Amelia Syndrome, a rare disorder characterized by the absence of all four limbs. At the age of ten, he attempted suicide but lived. Eventually, after years of feeling alone and worthless, he had an epiphany while reading an article about a disabled man who refused to let his physical limitations dictate his life. Nick says that it was at that moment he realized he had the ability to take control of his life. Instead of looking at everything he lacked, he decided to look at everything he had. I am moved to tears when I hear Nick say things like:

"You should never live according to what you lack."

"I was never crippled until I lost hope."

"There is one thing better than going to heaven, and that is to encourage at least one other person to go with me."

Such courage, such resilience, such focus, such strength, such grace—in the toughest of times—these qualities are what the Lord uses in us to inspire others.

The apostle Paul reminded us of the brilliance of grace and the ability each of us has to shine with the light of Christ throughout any season we find ourselves in:

But he answered me, "My grace is always more than enough for you, and my power finds its full expression through your weakness." So I will celebrate my weaknesses, for when I'm weak I sense more deeply the mighty power of Christ living in me. So I'm *not defeated* by my weakness, but delighted! For when I feel my weakness and endure mistreatment—when I'm surrounded with troubles on every side and face persecution *because of my love* for Christ—I am made yet stronger. For my weakness becomes a portal to God's power. (2 Corinthians 12:9–10 TPT)

No matter if we find ourselves in a summer season (because success brings its own set of challenges) or whether we are in deep winter (experiencing those long and often frustrating silent seasons), we find our strength in the golden thread of hope that God is with us.

A BEAUTIFUL GRACE

It can be tempting to look at all the things that are not quite right in life, all the areas that need work, and all the broken pieces that need restoring. But this beautiful grace we receive to stand in *His* strength is the glory of God at work in our midst. Learning to hand over the reins of your life to the Lover of your soul, especially when you simply don't understand the reason for the season you are in, this is truly one of the great arts of flourishing in your faith—and a measure of maturity.

Matthew Henry, a great theologian of the Christian faith, said:

When God does not take away our troubles and temptations, yet, if he gives grace enough for us, we have no reason to complain. Grace signifies the good-will of God towards us, and that is enough to enlighten and enliven us, sufficient to strengthen and comfort in all afflictions and distresses. His strength is made perfect in our weakness. Thus his grace is manifested and magnified. When we are weak in ourselves, then we are strong in the grace of our Lord Jesus Christ; when we feel that we are weak in ourselves, then we go to Christ, receive strength from him, and enjoy most the supplies of Divine strength and grace.[2]

Remember that when the apostle Paul wrote of strength in weakness, he was not talking about simply having a tough day. Rather, he was speaking of being grossly and unfairly treated, of suffering unimaginable hardships (often due to the actions of others), of chronic physical pain, and of feeling helpless and unable to do anything in the natural to turn a situation around. He is referring to seasons that by all appearances are hopeless, with no light visible at the end of the tunnel.

We all have areas of weakness in our lives. Maybe you have serious temptations that you wrestle with. Maybe you feel at times that these temptations are too strong for you to overcome. Maybe you have a weakness for gossip, or maybe there is a sickness in your body that is debilitating you in every way, and life seems unfair as you battle with prolonged physical weakness. Maybe you have been out of work for a long time, and just getting out to go to another interview feels like it will tip you overboard.

Our world has quite the dysfunctional relationship with weakness. We learn to self-medicate at the drop of a hat any weak feelings we experience. We "fill" our aging faces, erasing any wrinkles that we might see as a weakness. We work out at a ridiculous pace and go on the latest fad diet in order to achieve perfect bodies. We lie about our ages the older we get—as if this will somehow fool others into thinking we are younger. We even throw away and replace possessions if we discover the slightest imperfection. Some people have departed the faith, as they see it as a confession of weakness in this modern age.

We could be called the "throw-away generation," and because of this mind-set, our world can tend to treat precious people like this, too, especially those we see as too complex or too broken. I saw recently a short news piece about a celebrity having a rash on her legs—and this slight blemish made the nightly news! Lord, help us all if that is something we consider to be "newsworthy"!

NO MORE "PRETEND" LIFE

Jesus was not intimidated by weakness. In fact, He moved around His world as God wrapped in human flesh, strengthening people in their weakness, gathering to Himself the weak ones, the marginalized, and the forgotten of the world.

Whereas the rulers of the day saw those kinds of people as beneath them, Jesus saw them as individuals needing hope in their hopeless situations, needing life where there was death. He saw their need, and then He went about meeting it. He quoted a passage from Isaiah 61 when He announced His "mission statement" in a service at the synagogue:

> "The Spirit of the Lord is on me,
>> because he has anointed me
>> to proclaim good news to the poor.
> He has sent me to proclaim freedom for the prisoners
>> and recovery of sight for the blind,
> to set the oppressed free,
>> to proclaim the year of the Lord's favor."
>
> (LUKE 4:18–19 NIV)

While I was typing these words, our church was in the middle of preparations for our Easter services. In the midst of the renovations, I noticed the most beautiful steel crosses being built for our campuses. They were intricately welded and crafted to an extremely high quality. And then I noticed one of the young men responsible for these amazing creations. He had lived a tough life on the streets, yet slowly but surely he is seeing Jesus turn his life around. Rather than sit and wallow in the mistakes and defeats and hardships he encountered in his past, he has chosen again and again to serve others, to bring what he can to the feet of the Lord. Now his soul is being restored gracefully and completely as he fuels his spirit by serving others in his own season of weakness.

We go to such great lengths to polish our lives and pretend that any weak areas we might be experiencing are actually okay—or that they don't even exist. But Jesus wholeheartedly continues to say to each of us, "Come as you are!" His strength is made perfect *in* our weakness—not apart from our weakness.

With this amazing invitation from our Lord, then, why would we ever settle for a pretend life? Pretending is utterly exhausting. And yet the beauty of God's love is that wherever cracks appear in our lives, wherever things break apart that demonstrate our weakness, it's this very brokenness that attracts His great grace and mercy, for there is nothing about our lack that repels Him.

The Bible sets a high standard for how we should respond when we find ourselves in a weakened state. When we have been unfairly treated or when we simply feel unseen, when our souls are crying out for wholeness, Paul told us exactly what to do: "When reviled, we bless; when persecuted, we endure; when slandered, we forgive." And then he added, "We have been made as the filth of the world, the off-scouring of all things" (1 Corinthians 4:12–13 NKJV). In other words, this kind of response to hardship or harsh seasons will seem weak and feeble to those who don't understand, but as we respond in humility we experience His grace and power in the moment and as a taste of eternity.

He is with us on our mountaintops. He is also with us in our valleys, in all our sufferings. Oh, the sweet and powerful presence of God! David described it as the safest dwelling place in the universe, and truly the only safe dwelling place, for it alone lasts from everlasting to everlasting:

> Lord, you have been our dwelling place throughout all generations. Before the mountains were born or you brought forth the whole world, from everlasting to everlasting you are God. (Psalm 90:1–2 NIV)

YOUR THORN IN THE FLESH

Paul wrote about a "thorn in his flesh" or his "impossible situation." Paul prayed that God would take it away—"three times I pleaded with the Lord," and yet the Lord answered, "My power is made perfect in weakness" (2 Corinthians 12:8, 9 NIV).

Paul was begging that God would take the thorn away, and yet the Lord essentially said no, because His power was being made perfect in this weakness. In other words, God had a purpose to do something in Paul and through Paul by what was happening to Paul. And He says the same thing to us today. What the enemy meant for evil, God can always turn around for good. Through it all, God is at work to see His perfect will worked out in us. This is not the answer we always want to hear, though. We want a fast-acting prayer; we want the money to come in right away; we want a course of antibiotics to clear up the issue; we want that aggravating person simply out of our lives.

What is the purpose of such seasons in life? Why are our situations so intense at times? Maybe your questions include some of the following:

Why can't I find a job?
Why am I trapped in this awful marriage?

55

Why did my mother get cancer?

Why do some of my friends struggle to have children when
    other people in this world don't think twice about
    aborting a child?

Why does it feel like nothing is working out in my life?

Why is God asking me to extend myself to others in the midst
    of my own struggles?

I have learned to allow my questions to lead me back to the
sovereignty of God's plans and the way each of us is woven into His
redemptive plan for humanity. It is the power of God at work *in*
and *through* our very real lives that brings ultimate glory to God as
we serve Him and trust Him no matter what. When we are looking
for ways to bring the love of Christ to others, our weaknesses lose
their power to control us.

Charles Spurgeon wrote the following words of comfort many
years ago, but they still hold powerful truth for us today:

> Where God's arms are, He is at work, and He is at work accomplish-
> ing His purposes of grace.
>
>   The text (Deuteronomy 33) speaks of everlasting arms—
> that is a strength that never fails and never turns aside from the
> purpose to which it has bound itself. O child of God, down deep
> where you cannot see it, the divine power of the eternal Godhead
> is always at work for you! The arms of God are busy on your
> behalf! He has made them bare to show Himself strong in your
> defense! You can be sure of this! God has a purpose of love to all
> who believe in Him—and that purpose of love shall stand fast to
> all eternity! Whatever changes there may be in the appearance
> of this world and in the great universe of which it forms a part,
> there shall be no change in the infinite resolve of God to bless
> His people and preserve them to the end. Why, believer, be of
> good comfort, and say to yourself, "At the bottom of everything

that happens to me, there is the immutable purpose of God and God, Himself, working it out!"

The apostle Paul prayed until he got the word from the Lord that he sought—and until his heart truly trusted in the goodness of God in his situation. Just as Paul did, pray and keep praying. Ask and keep asking. God does not delight in your suffering. But God does use the suffering in our lives to show us more of Himself, more of His strength in our weakness.

And so we stand and we pray. When we resist the enemy, the Word says that he will flee from us (James 4:7). I experienced that profoundly during the time when I was sick and confused about the "thorn in my side." When battling cancer, I discovered that God was actually blessing *me* with a new group of amazing people who came into my life when I needed them the most. I found them in that dreadful yet hopeful world that is the belly of a hospital cancer ward. As the presence of God continued to surround us and as we fought our battles in Him and with Him, I learned the incredible truth that if *we* are willing, *He* will *still* use us—no matter what is going on in our own lives. He is greater than all circumstances, including cancer! Walking through cancer treatment actually gave me a pass into some people's worlds where I had previously had no authority.

All we need is to be willing for the Lord to use us. While we are broken, while we are hurting, all God is looking for is someone who is willing to stand with Him. While we may discount ourselves in inevitable seasons of hardship, the grace of God will be magnified. We will become more attractive to others as we exhibit grace in weakness. Our spirits will draw even the most cynical and resistant into our lives!

I love Bible stories that highlight everyday people, people God chose to use, who were foolish by the world's standards, but who, as they yielded their lives for His purposes, were made beautiful by the Lord—in His way and in His time. Seriously, would you send a teenager to fight a giant? Would you use a murderer to lead your people from bondage? God, in His grace, is audacious to do just that!

God's purpose in our weakness and seasons of struggle is ultimately to glorify the grace and the power of His Son. Jesus spoke directly into the heart of Paul in the words: "My grace is sufficient for you, for my power is made perfect *in* weakness" (2 Corinthians 12:9 NIV, emphasis mine). God's design for our lives is to make of us a showcase for Jesus' power, not by getting rid of all our weaknesses, but by giving us the strength to endure them—and even the ability to find great joy in the midst of our suffering.

THE GIFT OF SHARING HIS SUFFERINGS

And so, what is our rightful response to suffering within the framework of our lives? A dear friend said to me one day, while I was really scared during a chemo treatment, "I guess it is an amazing gift to be sharing in the sufferings of Christ." I had never thought of the cancer experience like that before. But I must say I found a beauty in my times of suffering. I discovered that when everything else is stripped away, it comes down to this: the most wonderful, awesome, incredible aspect of life is *to know Christ and to make Him known.*

Nothing else matters. I'm not sure I could have ever prayed so in unison with Paul had it not been for my affliction.

But whatever things were gain to me, those things I have counted as loss for the sake of Christ. More than that, I count all things to be loss in view of the surpassing value of knowing Christ Jesus my Lord, for whom I have suffered the loss of all things, and count them but rubbish so that I may gain Christ, and may be found in Him, not having a righteousness of my own derived from the Law, but that which is through faith in Christ, the righteousness which comes from God on the basis of faith, that I may know Him, and the power of His resurrection and the fellowship of His sufferings, being conformed to His death; in order that I may attain to the resurrection from the dead.

Not that I have already obtained it or have already become perfect, but I press on so that I may lay hold of that for which also I was laid hold of by Christ Jesus. Brethren, I do not regard myself as having laid hold of it yet; but one thing I do: forgetting what lies behind and reaching forward to what lies ahead, I press on toward the goal for the prize of the upward call of God in Christ Jesus. (Philippians 3:7–14 NASB)

The deepest need that you and I have in our times of weakness and adversity is not necessarily quick relief. Instead it is the well-grounded confidence that anything happening to us that is causing our weakness has already been overcome at the cross. The grace and power that held Jesus to the cross, and kept Him there until the work of love was done, are available to us all.

This is the pure golden strand of grace that God is weaving into each of our lives: more of Him, less of me.

6

THE POWER OF
THE TABLE

*Like the sacramental use of water and bread and
wine, friendship takes what's common in human
experience and turns it into something holy.*
—EUGENE H. PETERSON, *LEAP OVER A WALL*

ONE OF THE VERY FIRST PIECES OF FURNITURE MARK AND I
purchased as a married couple was a kitchen table. It came from
an antique store (a.k.a. "junk store") not far from where we lived.
Crammed full of other people's old and disregarded junk, the store
was filled with treasures for this newlywed couple. Amazingly, we
still have that table today. I don't think I could ever part with it.
It's still incredibly useful and precious as it's now usually occupied
by my grandchildren and all their projects and activities.

Growing up I simply loved being around anything to do with family. I had great dreams of a large kitchen table where we would all gather and eat and dream and spend many hours with each other and with other friends and family members who would come over and eat with us.

That was not always my childhood experience, but that vision became the prophetic nature of my kitchen table in my marriage with Mark and the raising of our children—to this day!

Over the years we had to buy an even bigger table to accommodate the growing number of people who gathered with us as we intentionally opened our home as part of our ministry to the people around us and as our family mission to have an open door for those who need *home*. Our kitchen table truly has become, as one of my girlfriends put it, the "central nervous system" of our home.

My very gracious husband, who is by nature someone who needs space and quiet to be refreshed, has taught me the art of finding the one who would normally get lost in a big bunch of people and noise and chatter, and finding a quiet corner to go deep in conversation. We allow the pull of the table to not only give life to the many, but also bring life to the one. This golden thread of hope through relationship has been one that my soul continues to treasure, as we were all designed to do life with others. I love some solitude; in fact I create well that way, but I also create well with others.

On a personal level I think I am like many in the way I need some alone time to simply be with Jesus and hear Him speak to me. I actually enjoy my own company! But I have noticed the pattern in my life when I have become tangled in knots emotionally or overthought different scenarios to the point of distraction. It is almost invariably when I have isolated myself from the grace of others. There is an unhealthy alone time when I water the wrong thoughts with the tears of self-pity. This is when God, through my kitchen table—the pull of doing life *with* others—woos me back to a place of comfort and hope.

THE LORD'S TABLE

I find it interesting that the same kind of pull I have toward my table, Jesus Himself had toward a certain table in the Scriptures. A physical table is not actually the point. But creating *value* around intentional time to sit with each other, to listen, to respond, to break bread, to laugh, or to cry is the point. For me, my kitchen table invites me into this space frequently and freely.

We have been given a precious picture in God's Word when, just before Jesus' greatest suffering, He *gathered* His disciples around the table and He *broke bread*.

In other words, He pulled together His precious friends (and one enemy). He gave thanks to His Father, and in doing so, He continued His personal preparation for what would ultimately be the greatest moment in all of history:

> Then came the preparation day of Unleavened Bread on which the Passover lamb had to be sacrificed. So Jesus sent Peter and John, saying, "Go and prepare the Passover meal for us, so that we may eat it." They asked Him, "Where do You want us to prepare it?" He replied, "When you have entered the city, a man carrying an earthen jar of water will meet you; follow him into the house that he enters. And say to the owner of the house, 'The Teacher asks, "Where is the guest room in which I may eat the Passover with My disciples?"' Then he will show you a large upstairs room, furnished [with carpets and dining couches]; prepare the meal there." They left and found it just as He had told them; and they prepared the Passover.
>
> When the hour [for the meal] had come, Jesus reclined at the table, and the apostles with Him. He said to them, "I have earnestly wanted to eat this Passover with you before I suffer; for I say to you, I will not eat it again until it is fulfilled in the kingdom of God." (Luke 22: 7–16 AMP)

Jesus Himself eagerly desired to be with His friends, and together they gathered around *purposed* food, that is, not just for their bodies, but food that was meant to nourish their souls and their spirits. I love the picture of Jesus reclining, perfectly at ease in the moment.

And so they shared in the service of Communion together, a spiritual meal that *prepared* all of them for the upcoming days.

The days in which we live, when many of us mistake busyness for purpose, and followers for friends, it is important that we have a sacred place where we can gather with others. We need to be able to share time, food, prayer, laughter, and challenges with just a few people or more. We need a place where our families and loved ones know they can come and relax in our presence. It does not have to be a pristine presence, but it needs to be a place that represents *life with others, and a place where you are free to be yourself.*

Some of you may not have a home where you can make this happen, but you may have a favorite coffee place or restaurant, or some place in the beautiful outdoors where you can sit, relax, and simply *be.*

At the kitchen table in my house—or while sitting at my kitchen bench—people feel free to walk in and pull up a chair while I put on the coffee (or they do!), and that place of safety immediately brings security and the sense of *selah*, and an ease around conversation begins.

WELCOME AT THE TABLE

Over the years, my kitchen table has been filled with sewing machines, painting projects, coloring books, pages filled with song lyrics, fresh flowers, cookie dough, and cookbooks, and women's magazines—and more homework than you'd ever like to imagine!

But what I've loved the most as my family and friends have

learned how to work together is that we've learned how to talk over the kitchen table.

Part of building a family is learning how to work together, how to be quiet together and how to be noisy together, depending on what is appropriate for the occasion.

Writing out party invitations, addressing hundreds of thank-you notes over the years, poring over kids' birthday cake recipes, planning great meals and actually cooking *terrible* meals—throughout all of it, our kitchen table has been the backdrop to many learning opportunities.

Brené Brown, a professor of social work whose major study has been conducted around vulnerability in society, had this to say about our deepest relationships: "Connection is the energy that is created between people when they feel seen, heard, and valued, when they can give and receive without judgment."[1]

With our kids and our friends and our spouses, it is so beneficial if we can create a space where there can be vulnerability, a sense of openness and honesty, without the pressure of having the perfect answer, and without the threat of experiencing an immediate rebuttal.

Such is the beauty of the kitchen table, where we have permission to be ourselves with each other. A sweet friend sent me a saying that has become one of my favorites: *Let's build longer tables and not higher fences.*

Oh, my heart.

Are people welcome at *your* table? Jesus taught profoundly around the topic of the Great Banquet:

When one of those at the table with him heard this, he said to Jesus, "Blessed is the one who will eat at the feast in the kingdom of God."

Jesus replied: "A certain man was preparing a great banquet and invited many guests. At the time of the banquet he sent his servant to tell those who had been invited, 'Come, for everything is now ready.'

"But they all alike began to make excuses. The first said, 'I have just bought a field, and I must go and see it. Please excuse me.'

"Another said, 'I have just bought five yoke of oxen, and I'm on my way to try them out. Please excuse me.'

"Still another said, 'I just got married, so I can't come.'

"The servant came back and reported this to his master. Then the owner of the house became angry and ordered his servant, 'Go out quickly into the streets and alleys of the town and bring in the poor, the crippled, the blind and the lame.'

"'Sir,' the servant said, 'what you ordered has been done, but there is still room.'

"Then the master told his servant, 'Go out to the roads and country lanes and compel them to come in, so that my house will be full. I tell you, not one of those who were invited will get a taste of my banquet.'" (Luke 14:15–24 NIV)

We all have times where we feel we are simply too busy to come and sit at someone else's table to share their lives and experiences with them—or to even think about making room for another at our own kitchen table. As pastors we find people in all walks of life who are simply lonely. Many have no "village" to turn to, no communal table to feel welcome at. This challenges me to the core. In the developing world, many have very little in the way of worldly possessions, but the village is strong. They share food, resources, parenting advice, and the table. Even if the table is a floor, they share life together there. On such travels, I have always been welcomed to come and just be part of the family vibe. And when food is scarce and water is muddied, they always wait until the guests have eaten as a sign of honor, and then they eat what is left. Super humbling to say the least. And the lessons our family has learned through experiences like this are timeless and of eternal significance.

Back when we were a family of four, I remember thinking, *There's still room at our table for more!* We tried to adopt a little boy. Our hearts broke when just before we were to take him home, government policy changed, and we had to yield to a decision taken out of our hands. Then we lost a long-awaited baby through miscarriage. Our hopes were dashed again. But after a long wait, the day came when we finally welcomed Zoe Jewel into the world. There was such a sense of completion in knowing the chair that had been empty at our table for so long would now be filled.

But we weren't done. I ended up buying more chairs. And then more chairs. There's still room at our table!

MAKE ROOM!

May I encourage you today to make some room in your heart and in your mind, at your kitchen bench, in your church, in your life group, or in your friendship circle—for others? Open yourself up to new possibilities in your life, new people to love, new people to learn from. We were meant to nourish other people and to be nourished by others. To *nourish* means so much more than just eating in the physical realm; it means to feed, to encourage, to nurture, to help something develop spiritually and emotionally and relationally.

Theologian N. T. Wright said: "The church exists primarily for two closely correlated purposes: to worship God and to work for his kingdom in the world. . . . The church also exists for a third purpose, which serves the other two: to encourage one another, to build one another up in faith, to pray with and for one another, to learn from one another and teach one another, and to set one another examples to follow, challenges to take up, and urgent tasks to perform. This is all part of what is known loosely as *fellowship*."[2]

Some of the most valuable times of fellowship happen as we break bread with others at our well-worn kitchen tables. It's time to declutter the space, open the door of your home and the door of your heart, and simply say, "There's a place for you at my table."

We learn this from the best. Jesus eats with everyone.

TRANSFORMED
BY HOPE

*The Hebrew term for hope literally means "a cord,
as an attachment." Every one of us is hanging
on to something or someone for security . . . if it's
someone or something other than God alone, you're
hanging on by a thread—the wrong thread.*
—BETH MOORE, *WHISPERS OF HOPE*

WHEN YOU START RESEARCHING THE BIBLICAL MEANING OF THE word *hope*, you get a clearer picture of God's heart for all people. The word is used to express "to trust in, to wait for, to look for, to desire something or someone, or to expect something beneficial in the future." References to this word are woven throughout

Scripture and describe a connection to a firm foundation that brings confidence to the situation—any situation.

At our church, Hope Unlimited Church, we say that hope has a name, and His name is Jesus. Some of our best friends have the last name of Hope. Our global outreach program is called HopeGlobal, the nickname for our church is HopeUC. We take the letters that spell *hope* and say Helping Other People Everywhere. Yes, I can confidently say that our "brand" is hope, but so much more important and in full reality, our default position, our passion, our purpose truly is hope. We hope in Christ, who is the anchor for our souls.

It is because of God's great golden strand of mercy at work in our hearts that He has made it possible for us to be made new, born again into a living hope: "Blessed be the God and Father of our Lord Jesus Christ! According to his great mercy, he has caused us to be born again to a living hope through the resurrection of Jesus Christ from the dead" (1 Peter 1:3 ESV).

RESURRECTION HOPE

The picture we have of Jesus in the Garden of Gethsemane is a difficult one to imagine: our Savior sweat drops of blood before He was to be separated from the Father for the one and only time in all eternity. As Jesus gave up His life for us, He traded the worst day in human history for the "living hope" that we find ourselves thriving within today. Even as the earth turned dark, time stood still, and creation wept on that Good Friday, the living hope continued to echo through the air. Resurrection promise was on its way.

The golden thread of living hope weaves itself throughout the Word of God and weaves itself into our hearts continually through Jesus' great sacrifice.

Dear friend, throughout any season in your life in which you are being stretched and tested, always remember Jesus' words as He surrendered to the Father's will: "Not My will, but Yours, be done" (Luke 22:42 NKJV). He *is* our hope. He is our confident Hope. It was through Jesus' death that new life would spring forth.

Hope is one of the three great theological virtues that Paul wrote about in 1 Corinthians 13—in addition to love and faith. Father Raniero Cantalamessa wrote:

> They are like three sisters. Two of them are grown and the other is a small child. They go forward together hand in hand with the child hope in the middle. Looking at them it would seem that the bigger ones are pulling the child, but it is the other way around; it is the little girl who is pulling the two bigger ones. It is hope that pulls faith and love. Without hope everything would stop.[1]

The challenge of walking in this new and living hope is that somewhere along the way, it will always require surrender. And sometimes we get stuck there. Hope deferred, like unfulfilled promises, really does cause our hearts to become quite ill (Proverbs 13:12). But it's good to remember that without Jesus' death and His surrender to His Father's will, the new resurrection life could not be ushered in. Jesus said He came to bring life *and* life in all its fullness (John 10:10). In long seasons of waiting, stand and declare, stand and sing it out, stand and with every fiber of your being shout that Jesus *is* your living hope, active and at work, that He is the hope of all our hearts, the hope of all the world. At the end of every church service at HopeUC, we speak the following blessing over our church family as they prepare to go into their world. The words come from Romans 15:13:

> I pray that God, the source of hope, will fill you completely with joy and peace because you trust in him. Then you will overflow with confident hope through the power of the Holy Spirit. (NLT)

This source of hope and this confident hope that is promised to us is made robust in our souls as we continue to lean into and trust the nature of God. There is newness of life everywhere. And this hope in Christ breathes the newness into life every minute of every hour in our lives. This is the beauty of our life in Christ; it is protected through the power of the Holy Spirit: "Therefore, if anyone is in Christ, he is a new creation. The old has passed away; behold, the new has come" (2 Corinthians 5:17 ESV).

Jesus' empty tomb is our forever reminder of the power that a new day can bring. Hope is here. A new beginning. A new life. As Jesus left the tomb as our resurrected Savior, He established forever a glorious future.

And He has taught you to let go of the lifestyle of the ancient man, the old self—life that was corrupted by sinful and deceitful desires that spring from delusions. Now it's time to be made new by every revelation that's been given to you and to be transformed as you embrace the glorious Christ-within as your new life and live in union with Him! God has re-created you all over again in His perfect righteousness, and you now belong to Him in the realm of true holiness.

TRANSFORMED BY HOPE

Allowing God to transform us as we embrace His ways of doing things can be both scary and exhilarating. Whether you are new on this journey of faith or you have been following Jesus for a long time, allowing His creative and perfect nature to work His will and plan in your life is an exciting part of the golden thread of hope.

C. S. Lewis explained the transforming power of hope in this way:

Hope is one of the Theological virtues. This means that a continual looking forward to the eternal world is not (as some modern people think) a form of escapism or wishful thinking, but one of the things a Christian is meant to do. It does not mean that we are to leave the present world as it is. If you read history you will find that the Christians who did most for the present world were just those who thought most of the next. The Apostles themselves, who set on foot the conversion of the Roman Empire, the great men who built up the Middle Ages, the English Evangelicals who abolished the Slave Trade, all left their mark on Earth, precisely because their minds were occupied with Heaven. It is since Christians have largely ceased to think of the other world that they have become so ineffective in this.[2]

Did you catch that? When we are transformed by hope, we are enabled to transform the world around us.

I will never forget the looks on each of my children's faces when they were baptized. They each waited until they were old enough to understand what they were doing, and then they made a public declaration of their faith. Amy glowed with thanksgiving. She is my determined but gentle soul, with enough empathy in that precious heart of hers to change the world. She had carefully and prayerfully thought through her decision, and from that day forward, a new and confident hope has shone brightly through her life.

Chloe was so overwhelmed at a baptism service she was attending one night that she jumped up and said, "I need to be baptized!" And right there, spur-of-the-moment, hope was like a firecracker in her, and she went all in. Her baptism decision was no less radical or meaningful, but it had less of a buildup.

And Zoe, well, her sisters baptized her in a moment I will always remember. It was in the midst of a hard season for our family, but it was a rich season in our faith journey. And Zoe's confident hope has been like a crown of florals upon her head throughout all of it, blooming beautifully despite her own doubts and fears.

This is resurrection life: walking away from the old, leaving behind the things that contain or corrupt, the things that make up your own regrets or burdens. The old is made new. Hope is made alive. We give up trying to live up to perfection, but we choose to walk in hope, to walk in love, to walk in the power of the Holy Spirit knowing that we are free, highly favored, and protected.

As we gaze into eternity with a confident hope, we are made new in the here and now.

A RIDICULOUSLY GENEROUS HOPE

If we sat at the table and shared, each of us would need an eternity to share the reasons we have a confident hope in Christ.

Experiencing a totally transformed life

Being set free from guilt and shame through the power of forgiveness

Rejoicing in a healed relationship

Sensing the Holy Spirit in your heart and knowing God is with you

Gaining incredible insight and wisdom while reading a Scripture passage

Receiving a specific answer to a specific prayer

Being healed or having someone you love tremendously to be healed in mind or body or spirit

All of us can remember a time we needed mercy. Then we experienced exactly what God promised in His Word: "The steadfast love of the LORD never ceases; his mercies never come to an end; they are new every morning; great is your faithfulness. 'The LORD is my portion,' says my soul, 'therefore I will hope in him'" (Lamentations 3:22–24 ESV).

This hope we have in Him can be difficult to comprehend and difficult to explain. How can the almighty God give so much, care so much, and bless so much for *me*?

But this is the miracle of hope. It is beautiful. It is surprising. It is just what you and I need.

Put your trust in Him and watch hope burst to life in you. His light overcomes any darkness.

> In the beginning was the Word, and the Word was with God, and the Word was God. He was in the beginning with God. All things were made through him, and without him was not any thing made that was made. In him was life, and the life was the light of men. The light shines in the darkness, and the darkness has not overcome it. (John 1:1–5 ESV)

I have this hope because I have seen and known the miracle-working power of God in my life a thousand times and more. And He is at work making all things new all the time. This is such great hope to hold onto.

Are you holding on? If this is a season of struggle for you, if the golden thread of His grace and love is difficult to perceive in your life right now, if you've taken God's work in your life for granted and not been mindful of His tender care for you, then read just a few short passages of Scripture—slowly, mindfully letting what may be very familiar words sink deep into your mind and soul:

> "He will wipe away every tear from their eyes, and death shall be no more, neither shall there be mourning, nor crying, nor pain anymore, for the former things have passed away." And he who was seated on the throne said, "Behold, I am making all things new." Also he said, "Write this down, for these words are trustworthy and true." (Revelation 21:4–5 ESV)

He put a new song in my mouth,
 a song of praise to our God.
Many will see and fear,
 and put their trust in the LORD.

(PSALM 40:3 ESV)

Jesus said to her, "I am the resurrection and the life. He who believes in Me, though he may die, he shall live. And whoever lives and believes in Me shall never die." (John 11:25–26 NKJV)

He reached down from heaven and rescued me;
he drew me out of deep waters.
He rescued me from my powerful enemies,
from those who hated me and were too strong for me.
They attacked me at a moment when I was in distress,
but the LORD supported me.
He led me to a place of safety;
he rescued me because he delights in me.

(PSALM 18:16–19 NLT)

When we cling to the golden thread of hope, God gives us a new song to sing; a prophetic declaration of things to come; a new way to express joy; a new way to fight our battles in Him; a new way to lift our heads high in the presence of our enemies. This hope is quite ridiculously generous when you really start to live it out. When we rise to worship, filled with a living hope, the songs we sing seem to take on greater meaning and impact and can reconstruct the sound of your soul. If your soul is tired, discouraged, confused, afraid, let God transform it as you sing out in hope.

His resurrection is what changed everything—everything in this world, and everything in each of our lives. One of the many reasons I am a Christian today is that the resurrection absolutely authenticates everything Jesus ever said and did. You can fight me on this or that in my theology, but you can never fight me on my experience. I know this hope that I have is my glory, the lifter of my head, my reason to fight for the right things in life, and the reason to be at peace in every situation.

And this hope that I know comes through the love of God, which He showers upon us moment by moment, since the beginning of time and on through all eternity. It is the most unfathomable love there is, yet it is here; it is available to be experienced in its fullness.

His love is perfect love, a totally giving and selfless love. John, the beloved follower of Christ, shared with us so simply and eloquently: "This is how we know what love is: Jesus Christ laid down his life for us" (1 John 3:16 NIV).

No matter what your opinion is about the love of God today, it doesn't change the fact that He loves you more than you could ever truly know. That is where I place my hope: His love.

HOPE LIFTS

On the previous page I asked you to read Psalm 18:16–19. As in Philippians 2:5–8, where Christ made Himself a servant, we discover that God is willing to "stoop down" so that we can be lifted up.

Stoop down? Lower Himself? God would do this? The Creator and Sustainer of all life? God's love is shown to us, not just in the stooping down but also in the lifting up. Jesus' *giving* His life for us is just the first half of the story. In His *resurrection*, all God's promises come to life!

Dear ones, this is what the golden thread of God's love actually looks like!

Love stoops down.
Love stops.

Love listens.

Love takes the time that is needed to foster relationships that matter.

And love lifts others up.

Love doesn't make people feel inferior to or "less than" itself.

Love pulls others up to its own level.

Love builds up.

Love edifies.

Love makes things new!

Our position in Christ, as sons and daughters of the most gracious God, is to serve and love others, to be builders of hope, following the example of our Lord and Savior.

Jesus' entire life was lived in service to a world who ultimately rejected Him. That's what made Him great. And following Him is what makes us great, as well. In opening our hearts to Jesus, we receive a new hope, a new beginning, a new sense of fulfillment that is completely unattainable outside of living our lives fueled by heaven-sent love. Serving others, giving our lives away, stooping down, lifting up—this is a love that is better than life, a love that will not let you go, a love that brings hope to every situation.

Hear the words of the Father for you, His golden thread of hope in Scriptures such as this weaving its way into your heart and your life: "Let the beloved of the LORD rest secure in him, for he shields you all day long, and the one the LORD loves rests between his shoulders" (Deuteronomy 33:12 NIV).

I have wonderful memories of my father throughout my childhood. But some of my very favorites are of the times when he would pick me up, put me high on his shoulders, and walk around; I was along for the ride. I felt so safe, so high above everything in our lives and our world. Since those days, I have watched my own husband do the same thing with our children and now with our grandchildren.

In the same way, the Lord loves for us to sit high, atop His shoulders. Safe on the shoulders of the Lord Jesus, resting high on the greatest display of love there will ever be. He stoops down, and He lifts us up. And as you abandon yourself to His love, confident hope continues to rise.

His golden grace and truth in my life truly does give me the firm grip I need to cling to hope. Yes, this is my very lifeline. My love for God has become deeper and yet simplified over many years. It is not conditional on what He gives or doesn't give to me, nor is it based on my emotions or affected by my negative situations. My love for Him is not dependent on my church or my friends. No, as I grow in my confidence of the great love of God toward me—toward us all, my faith in Him and His goodness has grown into a purer love. As He continually shows His love for me, this has become a love I trust and rest in.

Here are the lyrics from a song I wrote many years ago during a wonderful season of my life, a season where hope dawned over my soul in ways unspeakable and God's faithfulness was seen like the break of dawn over my life. Let the words wash over you.

My Hope

You are righteous,
Your love justice,
And those who honor You
Will see Your face,
I will arise and lift my eyes
To see Your majesty,
Your holiness,
And all I am will bless You.
[Chorus:]
My hope is in the Name of the Lord,
Where my help comes from,
You're my strength, my song,

My trust in the Name of the Lord,
I will sing Your praise,
You are faithful.

The golden thread of hope found in the Father's love is far greater than I ever imagined.

THE WILDERNESS

Behold, I will do a new thing,
Now it shall spring forth;
Shall you not know it?
I will even make a road in the wilderness
And rivers in the desert.
　　　　　　　　　—ISAIAH 43:19 NKJV

EVERY SEASON OF OUR LIVES IS MARKED BY THE GREAT, EXTRA-ordinary presence of God. He has planned our days for us ahead of time—and we know that He is guiding our steps through good times, through harder times, and through everything in between. The writer of the book of Ecclesiastes in the Old Testament, King Solomon, the wisest man who ever lived on this earth, said that there is a time for *everything*.

It is so easy to feel elated when we experience God on the mountaintop, in those "high experiences" that leave us almost intoxicated while being filled in His presence. Jesus' disciples experienced the same thing during their time with Him. There were experiences they had—including the Transfiguration, which occurred on a literal mountain—that left them completely awestruck; they no longer wanted to be part of this world. They had experienced heaven on earth:

> Six days later Jesus took Peter and the two brothers, James and John, and led them up a high mountain to be alone. As the men watched, Jesus' appearance was transformed so that his face shone like the sun, and his clothes became as white as light. Suddenly, Moses and Elijah appeared and began talking with Jesus. Peter exclaimed, "Lord, it's wonderful for us to be here! If you want, I'll make three shelters as memorials—one for you, one for Moses, and one for Elijah." (Matthew 17:1–4 NLT)

Peter wasn't alone in wanting to stay in the place where the light of heaven radiated over him. None of us wants to leave the mountaintop—but we do. We have to. It's part of life in this world. And even though we *always* have God's presence with us and in us, there will be many times when you may not feel God. But this is the life of faith, to believe in God and take Him at His word, to walk by faith and not by the things we see.

Yes, there are times we must journey through the valley.

IT IS WELL WITH MY SOUL

It's a song we all know and love, and many of us have heard the story that brought about its writing.

Horatio Spafford (1828–1888) was a wealthy Chicago lawyer

with a beautiful home, a lovely wife, and beloved children: four daughters and a son. He was also a devout Christian who loved God's Word. His circle of friends included Dwight L. Moody and Ira Sankey, well-known Christians of the day.

At the very height of his financial and professional success, Horatio and his wife, Anna, suffered the tragic loss of their young son. Shortly thereafter, on October 8, 1871, the Great Chicago Fire destroyed almost every real estate investment that Spafford had made.

Then, just two short years later, in 1873, Spafford scheduled a boat trip to Europe in order to give his wife and daughters time to recover from these multiple tragedies. He was planning to join Moody and Sankey on an evangelistic campaign in England, but he sent his wife and daughters ahead of him across the Atlantic. Several days later, he received notice that his family's ship had encountered a collision. All four of his daughters drowned; only his wife miraculously survived.

With a heavy heart, Spafford boarded the boat that would take him to his grieving wife in England. It was on this trip that he penned these incredible words: "When sorrow like sea billows roll; it is well, it is well with my soul."

The song was later published in 1876 by Philip Bliss, who composed the music, and Sankey. And here we are today, more than 150 years later, finding great comfort through the words, composed during a time of immense suffering and grief.

How can we as believers honestly say, "It is well with my soul," when the storms of life are blowing to such an extent? How can we say it and really mean it?

There is a story in the Bible that tells of this same spiritual fortitude in the face of immense grief. We don't know the main character's name, just where she lived. But her encounter with one of God's prophets keeps her memory alive today. Second Kings 4 (NLT) is where her story is told.

One day Elisha went to the town of Shunem. A wealthy woman lived there, and she urged him to come to her home for a meal. After that, whenever he passed that way, he would stop there for something to eat. (v. 8)

It is noteworthy that she had a heart of service and generosity.

She said to her husband, "I am sure this man who stops in from time to time is a holy man of God. Let's build a small room for him on the roof and furnish it with a bed, a table, a chair, and a lamp. Then he will have a place to stay whenever he comes by." (vv. 9–10)

Her love for God showed up in her extravagant love for His messenger! That obviously caught Elisha's attention and moved him to compassion for her.

One day Elisha returned to Shunem, and he went up to this upper room to rest. He said to his servant Gehazi, "Tell the woman from Shunem I want to speak to her." When she appeared, Elisha said to Gehazi, "Tell her, 'We appreciate the kind concern you have shown us. What can we do for you? Can we put in a good word for you to the king or to the commander of the army?'" (vv. 11–13)

This woman was extraordinary. She didn't bless Elisha for personal gain but because it was in her nature to love and bless others.

"No," she replied, "my family takes good care of me." (v. 13)

She definitely had Elisha's attention. Her selfless generosity so captured him that he knew there must be some way he could bless her in return.

Later Elisha asked Gehazi, "What can we do for her?" Gehazi replied, "She doesn't have a son, and her husband is an old man." (v. 14)

Now Elisha knew the secret pain of her heart.

"Call her back again," Elisha told him. When the woman returned, Elisha said to her as she stood in the doorway, "Next year at this time you will be holding a son in your arms!" (vv. 15–16)

Her response revealed years of longing.

"No, my lord!" she cried. "O man of God, don't deceive me and get my hopes up like that." (v. 16)

Even the most faithful servant of God can reveal doubts in the face of a long period of disappointment. But the prayer of her heart was answered.

But sure enough, the woman soon became pregnant. And at that time the following year she had a son, just as Elisha had said. (v. 17)

We would love it if the story ended here. But that's when tragedy struck this beautiful woman of faith.

One day when her child was older, he went out to help his father, who was working with the harvesters. Suddenly he cried out, "My head hurts! My head hurts!"

His father said to one of the servants, "Carry him home to his mother."

So the servant took him home, and his mother held him on her lap. But around noontime he died. She carried him up and laid him on the bed of the man of God, then shut the door and left him there. She sent a message to her husband: "Send one of the servants and a donkey so that I can hurry to the man of God and come right back." (vv. 18–22)

How many of us would quit right then? My prayers weren't answered. My situation is hopeless. But she persisted in her mighty faith.

"Why go today?" he asked. "It is neither a new moon festival nor a Sabbath."

But she said, "It will be all right."

So she saddled the donkey and said to the servant, "Hurry! Don't slow down unless I tell you to." (vv. 23–24)

My friends, when in a crisis, do as she did. She didn't hesitate or move slowly toward God. She ran there with all her might.

Elisha saw her from a distance and sent a servant running to find out the problem. Sounds a little like a story in Luke 15, doesn't it? There a loving father ran out to greet his prodigal son. The message in both stories is that we have a loving Father who watches for us.

As she approached the man of God at Mount Carmel, Elisha saw her in the distance. He said to Gehazi, "Look, the woman from Shunem is coming. Run out to meet her and ask her, 'Is everything all right with you, your husband, and your child?'"

But when she came to the man of God at the mountain, she fell to the ground before him and caught hold of his feet. Gehazi began to push her away, but the man of God said, "Leave her alone. She is deeply troubled, but the LORD has not told me what it is." (vv. 25–27)

In life's darkest moments, we can feel rejected by the world, but God will never push us away.

This woman's relationship with God was incredibly intimate and honest. In no way did she hold back in sharing the pain that was in her heart. She accepted the invitation to come boldly before the throne of God. Indeed, God wants us to come to Him with absolute honesty and transparency. He doesn't want platitudes; He wants us! That's when He is able to speak love and truth into our hearts.

> Then she said, "Did I ask you for a son, my lord? And didn't I say, 'Don't deceive me and get my hopes up'?"(v. 28)

What our miracle-working, all-powerful God did for this woman through Elisha was nothing short of amazing.

> Then Elisha summoned Gehazi. "Call the child's mother!" he said. And when she came in, Elisha said, "Here, take your son!" She fell at his feet and bowed before him, overwhelmed with gratitude. Then she took her son in her arms and carried him downstairs. (vv. 36–37)

What a story! And I *love* this woman in the Scriptures. Something inside of her was so passionate for God that she would have done anything to get close to Him! Not only that, but she was hospitable, giving, kind, and persuasive, and she consistently went out of her way for other people. She had a tremendous amount of faith! She is described in the Bible as a "great woman"—meaning that she was bold, mighty, and noble in her faith. She was a woman who would not take no for an answer.

But the words in the story that jumped out to me were the ones in which our persistent woman, when she was asked, "Is all well with you, your husband, your son?" she declared, "It is well." Wow!

NO MATTER WHAT

What is it about *your* soul that makes it possible for you to declare "It is well" even when all hell is breaking loose in your life? Even as one who finds it easy to sit on the bright side of life, this story really challenges me.

When I thought about Horatio Spafford and the losses he suffered before he penned the words of that beautiful hymn, and when I thought about this Shunamite woman and her declaration of hope, I realized that both of these people displayed so much faith! They believed not just in God at work in their circumstances—remember, Spafford's children perished, and the Shunamite woman's son was later saved—but they both displayed a faith that trusted in the love of God toward them—*no matter what*.

> It's a trust that secures the heart to the finished work of Christ.
> It's a trust that secures the soul to the Word and to every *promise* of God.
> It's a trust that declares hope over deep darkness and despair.
> It's a trust that vehemently believes that God works all things together for good.
> It's a trust that tethers the spirit to grace and not to works.

To be able to stand, feet firmly planted on the ground, and say "It is well" in all things is *not* a flippant kind of faith; it is actually faith that chooses to trust in God and His steadfast promises.

> Trust in the LORD with all your heart
> and lean not on your own understanding;
> in all your ways submit to him,
> and he will make your paths straight. (Proverbs 3:5–6 NIV)

It is a stubborn, relentless faith that *will not let go of God's promise for anything.*

Remember that God sees the beginning from the end, whereas we often get caught up in seeing the immediate circumstances of our situation.

What I also noticed about this amazing Shunamite woman is that she did not allow others to comment on her troubles as she clung to her faith in God—not even her husband! She put the dead boy onto the bed of the prophet; then she grabbed a donkey and told the servants not to slow down for anything. She stayed incredibly focused and she placed herself among people of faith.

King David is another example of a person who trusted God wholeheartedly, who believed in the Lord no matter what circumstances he found himself in:

> O God, you are my God;
> I earnestly search for you.
> My soul thirsts for you;
> my whole body longs for you
> in this parched and weary land
> where there is no water.
> I have seen you in your sanctuary
> and gazed upon your power and glory.
> Your unfailing love is better than life itself;
> how I praise you!
> I will praise you as long as I live,
> lifting up my hands to you in prayer.
> You satisfy me more than the richest feast.
> I will praise you with songs of joy.
> I lie awake thinking of you,

meditating on you through the night.
Because you are my helper,
I sing for joy in the shadow of your wings.
I cling to you;
your strong right hand holds me securely. (Psalm 63:1–8 NLT)

David wrote this psalm in the desert—a harsh place, with no water, a place where his physical means would be stretched to the limits. And not only was his body thirsty and hungry, but his very life was in danger. He was hiding out from his enemies, who sought to kill him. And so *fear* lurked around every corner.

We can learn so many valuable lessons from the wilderness. In his wilderness experiences, David established in his heart, yet again, that God was the Ruler of his heart. Not trouble, and not even success, would be his primary focus. First and foremost he prayed: "O God, You are my God." The Lord was not distant to David but close. David had a relationship of trust in his God. And even though there was a desert all around him, there was no desert to be found in his heart.

In this latest season of my life, in which death tried to swallow my victory, I have had to stay very disciplined and intentional in what I allow my mind to dwell upon, which people I hang around, where I place my energy, and whom and what I allow close to my heart.

Interestingly, just before I was diagnosed with breast cancer in December 2013, one of my dear girlfriends, Dianne, had a sign made for me that read: "It is well with my soul." Little did we know that four weeks later, I would be clinging to that phrase with all of my faith. This sign now hangs at the entry of our home, and whenever our family leaves the house and whenever we enter our home again, we are reminded that *it is well*.

We have had a long-term issue with stalkers too; we have had to move homes, change all our contacts various times, and this has brought great grief to our family. But as we walk in and out of our home now with the words IT IS WELL declared over the doorways, we remember that words have the power to create, and this creates a consistency of security in our souls.

During that season and ever since, I have intentionally placed myself around people of faith, and as always, I have been deeply rooted in the house of God. I am not retreating; I have not gotten mad at God. I have just enjoyed being around faith! Having the Word around me and in me all the time has made me so much stronger—and it has caused the song of my heart to keep flowing rather than drying up inside of me like an old, bitter, stagnant riverbed.

When the desert is trying to sing your song for you, part of being able to say "It is well" is based on how you have dug your own well in God. Every time you choose to put your absolute trust in God before you place any trust in your circumstances, you dig your own personal well a little bit deeper. And every time you choose to worship God rather than allow your worship to be silenced, you dig your well a little deeper in the desert.

Choose to worship—even when you just don't feel like it. That's the whole point. Worship will always help your heart to find its way back to God's throne. Sometimes you've just got to tell your soul what it needs, and you can do that through worshipping the Lord. Truthful, raw, and honest worship is one of the strongest ways to lead your soul to health. People have asked me why I did not just retreat and rest at home throughout my own challenging season. I have to wonder, *What would I have done at home, left to my own devices, thinking my own thoughts?* That would have been a disaster!

No, I needed to be around faith. I needed to be spending time in worship with my dear church family. I needed the fellowship of my worship team to help lead my soul in singing. And just like the Shunamite woman, I had to become disciplined about who I spent much time with. I simply don't have room anymore for vague comments or negativity. I need God's Word and His promises to be embedded into my spirit by the people around me.

Two times the Shunamite woman was asked, "Is it well?" and three times she answered, "It is well." And her son was brought back to life.

The Shunamite woman, Horatio Spafford, and King David all declared "It is well" *long before* things actually were well in their circumstances. All of us need to dig our own wells in God. Practicing thanksgiving in dark days is gutsy. Giving praise and thanks in the valley seasons causes us to remember again that this is a spiritual battle, not a natural one.

The days of our greatest blessings are often, if not always, hidden by the darkest of nights. And so we ask, and we keep on asking, and we keep on thanking God all the while for His goodness and provision in our lives. When you *know* that you are loved by God Himself, you can trust Him to do what He says He will do.

Why don't you challenge your soul—made up of your mind, will, and emotions—for when it is firmly planted in the Word of God, it will eventually find its way to say, "It is well."

So, how's *your* soul today?

I have had seasons when my soul was so tired that I could barely say "It is well" on the outside, and my comment had no genuine connection to what was happening on the inside of my heart. It has taken time and the great grace of God to allow my soul and my mind to become "authentic friends." My friend Alicia Britt Chole texted me the other day and said, "Grief is a funny thing, but one of the only ways for your heart and soul to stay connected." I am taking time to meditate on the depth of that phrase.

I've had to allow the voice of doubt, the stifled voice that questions everything, to be given airtime, so that with love and patience, the Holy Spirit could begin to redirect my thought process and practices. Rather than feel disqualified through my doubts, though, I have gone to the Word and dug another well in Christ while walking through the desert. There are no limits to the number of encounters God has waiting for us on a personal level through His Word.

When Isaac was faced with drought and trouble, the Lord spoke to him in a profound way:

> From there he went up to Beersheba. That night the LORD appeared to him and said, "I am the God of your father Abraham. Do not be afraid, for I am with you; I will bless you and will increase the number of your descendants for the sake of my servant Abraham."
>
> Isaac built an altar there and called on the name of the LORD. There he pitched his tent, and there his servants dug a well. (Genesis 26:23–25 NIV)

Isaac worshipped the Lord, pitched his tent, and dug another well that would remind him of the certainty of God's promises, and every time he drank from that well from then on, he would remember what God had spoken to him.

And we dig our wells the same way: we worship and pray, we find our thirst quenched even in desert times, and as we worship, we are reminded of the truth of God's presence in our lives. Our wells hold the depth of continued revelation of who God is to each of us.

The Holy Spirit will always minister to you in the desert spaces of your life. In fact, the Word tells us that when we are at our weakest, these times actually help to showcase God's goodness at its finest. Think of all the spaces that feel uncomfortable and full of questions, where your faith feels stretched to the limit, the trying seasons that have seemed so prolonged, and how overcoming them has seemed so impossible.

Oh, friend, let's lean into the realm of the Spirit, where God longs to meet with each of us, and by faith let's bring everything we have into His light. He is never surprised or disappointed. And He will breathe life into our dead situations again and again, and sometimes even allow something from your life to be removed. Trust is required, friends, in these desert seasons of prolonged dryness, so dig your well in God. This well will nourish you for the rest of your life, as His river on the inside of you finds its fullness of expression, flowing out to everyone around you, so that even when you don't understand, you can still genuinely say, "It is well."

FORGIVENESS

To be a Christian is to forgive the inexcusable,
because God has forgiven the inexcusable in you.
—C. S. LEWIS, *THE WEIGHT OF GLORY*

ALTHOUGH IT CAN BE DIFFICULT AT TIMES, MOVING INTO A NEW season is also filled with many exciting moments. Meeting new people (even though this makes introverts shudder!), walking into new possibilities, trying out new things, discovering new friendships, learning new places to take the family—the list goes on and on.

God had given us beautiful promises to hold on to, and I have journals filled with Scriptures the Holy Spirit etched into our hearts during those days when new was everywhere, like the following:

"Behold, My Servant, whom I uphold;
My Chosen One in whom My soul delights.
I have put My Spirit upon Him;
He will bring forth justice to the nations.
"He will not call out or shout aloud,
Nor make His voice heard in the street.
"A broken reed He will not break [off]
And a dimly burning wick He will not extinguish [He will not
        harm those who are weak and suffering];
He will faithfully bring forth justice.
"He will not be disheartened or crushed [in spirit];
[He will persevere] until He has established justice on the
        earth;
And the coastlands will wait expectantly for His law. . . .
"I am the LORD, that is My Name;
My glory I will not give to another,
Nor My praise to carved idols.
"Indeed, the former things have come to pass,
Now I declare new things;
Before they spring forth I proclaim them to you."
Sing to the LORD a new song,
Sing His praise from the end of the earth!
You who go down to the sea, and all that is in it,
You islands and coastlands, and those who inhabit them [sing
        His praise]!
Let the wilderness and its cities lift up their voices,
The villages where Kedar lives.
Let the inhabitants of Sela shout for joy,
Let them shout joyfully from the tops of the mountains.
Let them give glory to the LORD
And declare His praise in the islands and coastlands.
The LORD will go forth like a warrior,
He will stir up His zeal like a man of war;

He will shout out, yes, He will raise a war cry.
He will prevail [mightily] against His enemies.

(ISAIAH 42:1–4, 8–13 AMP)

As hard as it was to let go of the old things in our lives, God was busy making all things new—and His "new thing" was certainly alive and well in my spirit. It was like I could see the word *hope* being written across the Central Coast—where we now live and where our campuses began—and beyond. At times it was also as if I could literally feel we were surfing upon the surge of prayer that had been lifted up over this region for so many generations. It is such a joy and privilege to serve this community in any way we can.

Have you ever felt like your capacity was being enlarged at such a pace that you could almost hear it taking place? That is what that season was like. We were being stretched to the left and to the right, we were learning to work with new people, I was really missing all my friends, we found ourselves in new places—and I actually came to the very end of myself, even to the point of second-guessing our decisions during this period. I loved being *with* people as their pastor, being back in the hospitals and walking alongside people as they bravely journeyed through illness, watching people grow in their faith, championing other friends and leaders as they went out and made their own marks for Christ. I wept with people and laughed with people. We went back to the basics with our worship and creative teams. And since that time there has been a lot of fun along the way!

Throughout this entire period of time, I've had to relearn the art of surrender. This word, *surrender,* became a fresh part of my daily prayer: *Please, Lord, help me to surrender my ways, my learned behaviors, my preconceived ideas. Oh, that I would not get in the way of Your plans and purposes for my life and for the people I am called to serve.*

As I've said, the kindness of God also continued to lead me to Scriptures that confirmed His ever-present love for me. He was reassuring me that *just me being me* was enough for Him. As a chronic self-confessed "doer," this revelation continues to deepen and settle within my spirit. Oh, friend, when the love of God gets hold of you, there is no stopping what He will accomplish in and through you, by the power of the Holy Spirit and through your cooperation, your working in partnership with God's purposes.

> Through our faith, the mighty power of God constantly guards us until our full salvation is ready to be revealed in the last time. May the thought of this cause you to jump for joy, even though lately you've had to put up with the grief of many trials. But these only reveal the sterling core of your faith, which is far more valuable than gold that perishes, for even gold is refined by fire. Your authentic faith will result in even more praise, glory, and honor when Jesus the Anointed One is revealed.
>
> You love him passionately although you did not see him, but through believing in him you are saturated with an ecstatic joy, indescribably sublime and immersed in glory. For you are reaping the harvest of your faith—the full salvation promised you—your souls' victory! (1 Peter 1:5–9 TPT)

Surrendering our lives to God is by no means a light or casual choice to make. It is in this surrender, however, that we find true freedom. Every promise declared by God in His Word simply cannot fail, and He cannot lie. But when our lives are willfully out of sync with His will and His plan, we will find ourselves in trouble and in confusion. Letting go of control and yielding to God's higher ways becomes a genuine joy when you know that His love for you is so infinite—limitless or endless in space, extent, or size; impossible to measure or calculate. Your confidence in His plans for your life will only continue to grow as you surrender to Him.

I have been crucified with Christ; and it is no longer I who live, but Christ lives in me; and the life which I now live in the flesh I live by faith in the Son of God, who loved me and gave Himself up for me. (Galatians 2:20 NASB)

Then Jesus said to His disciples, "If anyone wishes to come after Me, he must deny himself, and take up his cross and follow Me. For whoever wishes to save his life will lose it; but whoever loses his life for My sake will find it." (Matthew 16:24–25 NASB)

I have found that my heart leans into surrender to the Lord more easily when I am in worship, in prayer, or in stillness. It's in this place of communion with Him that I continually hear God speak. He brings to attention the things I need to address in the deepest recesses of my heart, and He talks to me lovingly about my blind spots, all the while speaking His heart of love toward me. His words are like a continual stream of hope that He infuses into the core of my being.

> Consider and answer me, O LORD my God;
> light up my eyes, lest I sleep the sleep of death,
> lest my enemy say, "I have prevailed over him,"
> lest my foes rejoice because I am shaken.
> But I have trusted in your steadfast love;
> my heart shall rejoice in your salvation.
> I will sing to the LORD,
> because he has dealt bountifully with me.
>
> (PSALM 13:3–6 ESV)

There have been some interesting things revealed to my heart in these times. Some glorious truths were highlighted from heaven as "yes and amen," and they have since become part of my spiritual DNA. But there are also things to which I had become blind in my past. It's often hard to see your own pride creeping in or realize that buried unforgiveness has begun to grow like mold in the darkest corners of your heart. But these are the areas that need the security of His presence and the light of His love. As the psalmist said, "He has dealt bountifully with me." And He will also deal bountifully with you. This is why the Word of God reminds us that it's in His presence you'll find fullness of joy, for it's in His presence that you will understand, at the deepest of levels of your being, who you truly are *in* Christ.

One of the things that is very dear to me is loyalty—from my family and friends, in particular. I tend to give my heart away very slowly, but once you have it, you really have it. This way of living is walked out by millions of other people just like me on a daily basis. This may sound really noble, or maybe to some a bit intense, but this is me. The problem is that when your heart is broken, when trust has been abused or perhaps just not handled like you thought it should be handled, people like me tend to lock their hearts back down again. It's our natural instinct to try to avoid "soul destruction," and so we practice an unhealthy tendency to preserve our own sense of being. You can understand that surrendering my heart again and again to the Lord, including my thought processes, my ways, and my will, has been and always will be of monumental importance to the health of my soul, my body, and my spirit.

It was in this place of surrender that I felt the Holy Spirit speak to my heart very clearly. He said, "Daughter, you need to forgive." He reminded me of some things that I had locked away over decades, and to be honest I thought I had dealt with them, even things that went back to my teenage years. But you know, we serve a God who deals in truth, and here He was, highlighting parts of my soul that still needed a makeover.

How do you forgive when you feel you have been wronged? How do you forgive—*really* forgive—when the actual hurt is replayed over and over in your mind? How do you forgive actions that hurt you sometimes for decades, patterns of sin and destruction that seem to make the act of forgiveness too difficult to accomplish?

For a short period of time, holding on to unforgiveness almost feels good, kind of like eating junk food. It feels great for about five minutes—and then, well, you know. It doesn't feel so good an hour later. When your offense and unforgiving spirit feels justified, it becomes especially hard to let go. But when unforgiveness is undealt with, and when it festers for days, months, even years, it becomes like poison in your soul. And the one who is left emotionally crippled is *you*.

I have often talked about my cancer journey, the passage through pain that had no shortcuts, but I had a promise from God that He would *never* leave me nor forsake me as we walked together through the valley of the shadow of death. And then I received a surprise when I felt the Lord tug at my spirit and ask me to make some room in my heart. While I was busy fighting for my life, these were not the comforting words I was expecting to hear from heaven.

"How do I 'make room in my heart'?" I asked the Lord.

As I waited for God to answer this question, He started to show me people I needed to forgive. He showed me that there was too much clutter in my heart, clutter that was taking up space He had reserved for much clearer and higher thoughts and dreams.

Oh, how Jesus and I went on a long journey of decluttering the sacred spaces of my heart!

This was both painful and intentional, but every time a thought came up, I learned to ask God to give me the grace I needed to forgive, especially related to those things I did not understand. I prayed that my offender, too, would find the grace to forgive me if I had also been part of the wrongdoing.

"Teacher, which is the greatest commandment in the Law?"

Jesus replied: 'Love the Lord your God with all your heart and with all your soul and with all your mind.' This is the first and greatest commandment. And the second is like it: 'Love your neighbor as yourself. All the Law and the Prophets hang on these two commandments.' " (Matthew 22:36–40 NIV)

Wow! The Lord has told us that the two greatest commands He has given are these: to love the Lord with all your heart and *to love others as yourself*! Through this time of testing in my life, I became aware of how hard it is to love with *all* your heart when pieces of your heart have been cut off by hurt and disappointment.

Be kind and compassionate to one another, forgiving each other, just as in Christ God forgave you. (Ephesians 4:32 NIV)

Forgiveness ultimately brings you the freedom you need to truly love others—and to love yourself. Jesus told this parable to illustrate the power of forgiveness:

Then Peter came to Him and asked, "Lord, how many times will my brother sin against me and I forgive him and let it go? Up to seven times?" Jesus answered him, "I say to you, not up to seven times, but seventy times seven.

"Therefore the kingdom of heaven is like a king who wished to settle accounts with his slaves. When he began the accounting, one who owed him 10,000 talents was brought to him. But because he could not repay, his master ordered him to be sold, with his wife and his children and everything that he possessed, and payment to be made. So the slave fell on his knees and begged him, saying, 'Have patience with me and I will repay you everything.' And his master's heart was moved with compassion and he released him and forgave him [canceling] the debt. But that same slave went out and found one of his fellow slaves who owed him a hundred denarii; and he seized him and began choking him, saying, 'Pay what you owe!' So his fellow slave fell on his knees and begged him earnestly, 'Have patience with me and I will repay you.' But he was unwilling and he went and had him thrown in prison until he paid back the debt. When his fellow slaves saw what had happened, they were deeply grieved and they went and reported to their master [with clarity and in detail] everything that had taken place. Then his master called him and said to him, 'You wicked and contemptible slave, I forgave all that [great] debt of yours because you begged me. Should you not have had mercy on your fellow slave [who owed you little by comparison], as I had mercy on you?' And in wrath his master turned him over to the torturers (jailers) until he paid all that he owed. My heavenly Father will also do the same to [every one of] you, if each of you does not forgive his brother from your heart." (Matthew 18:21–35 AMP)

Jesus defined *forgiveness* right here in this story. Forgiveness is not simply a response to an emotion or feeling, and it is certainly not trying hard to forget, like many of us seem to think that it is. Trying hard to forget really only helps you remember! Instead, Jesus has defined *forgiveness* as our passing on to those who have sinned against us the grace and the mercy that we ourselves have received from God. And He instructs us not only to forgive a few times but to forgive again and again and again. Jesus was teaching Peter that how Peter forgave other people would reveal the work and the nature of Peter's God. Think about it this way: if Peter forgave other people up to seven times, then he was reflecting a God who forgives like human beings do.

But if Peter was to forgive other people seventy-seven times, then Peter was showing that he was responding to the work of Christ's love in him, and he would be showing the world that our God and His work in our lives gives us the power to forgive as only God forgives. This is *such* good news for us all! There is no hurt, there is no curse, there is no sin, and there is no disappointment that is too great for us to forgive, because if we are empowered by the Holy Spirit, we have been given the ability to forgive and release others from the debt that they owe to us—just as Jesus Himself has done for us!

All of this reveals the nature and character of the God we serve, the God who is alive within us! The Bible also tells us that forgiveness keeps the enemy of our souls from gaining an advantage or taking the upper hand over us. When you get lost in your own world of unforgiveness, it really does cause your eyes to be dulled to other things going on around you, leaving you vulnerable to the plans of the enemy.

> If you forgive anyone anything, I too forgive [that one]; and what I have forgiven, if I have forgiven anything, has been for your sake in the presence of [and with the approval of] Christ, to keep Satan from taking advantage of us; for we are not ignorant of his schemes. (2 Corinthians 2:10–11 AMP)

Paul told us to forgive as the Lord forgave us (Colossians 3). And so, as followers of Jesus, this becomes a commandment for us. And as hard as it may be, forgiveness is something that we all need to keep working at—as often as necessary to bring the release. Even if our feelings don't match up, we are still called to forgive.

I talk about Rwanda often, as God has placed her like a precious piece of homeland in my heart. Rwanda is a country that is lovingly known as the "heart of Africa." After the genocide that took place there in 1994, in which approximately one million precious people were systematically killed in the space of one hundred days—a bloody, heartless ethnic cleansing—the horror is still something I find very difficult to fathom. One people group believed that they were superior to another, and neighbors began to kill neighbors. Paul Kagame, who eventually became the president of this nation that is so close to our hearts, has said about Rwanda: "Until the *heart* of our land is healed, the body can't be fixed." He challenged his country with the need to offer forgiveness to one another; otherwise, as he said, "this tragedy will be how we are remembered."

If we try to live without forgiveness, we allow pride to become our stance in life. And we won't survive. We'll drown in our bitterness. You don't want your toughest memory to become the very thing that defines your life!

Chronic and sustained anger over a long period of time will put your body into the fight-or-flight mode, which results in numerous changes in your heart rate, your blood pressure, and your immune response. Those changes then in turn increase your risk for depression, heart disease, diabetes, and many other serious health conditions. Forgiveness, however, calms your stress levels, leading to improved health and numerous positive changes in heart rate, blood pressure, and immune response. Those changes then, in turn, decrease your risk of depression, heart disease, and diabetes, and all the other conditions caused by the fight-or-flight response. I also found out recently that a hug calms our nervous systems. Seriously, God is a genius!

And so, how can we become people who know how to forgive? We must learn, my friend, because, to be honest, our future and our children's futures depend on it!

Follow these steps found in Scripture to begin a pattern of forgiveness in your life: decide to forgive and depend on the Holy Spirit.

1. DECIDE TO FORGIVE

Decide to live as someone who keeps short accounts with others. Don't wait for your feelings to catch up with what you know to be right. Make the quality decision to forgive, and you will find that God will heal your soul as you continue to forgive. I found that over time, the sting that sometimes surfaced over seemingly small things, as I brought forgiveness, has actually completely disappeared, and now I can pray with genuine compassion.

> "And forgive us our debts, as we have forgiven our debtors [letting go of both the wrong and the resentment].
>
> "And do not lead us into temptation, but deliver us from evil. [For Yours is the kingdom and the power and the glory forever. Amen.]"
>
> "For if you forgive others their trespasses [their reckless and willful sins], your heavenly Father will also forgive you." (Matthew 6:12–14 AMP)

2. DEPEND ON THE HOLY SPIRIT

You cannot forgive without the power of the Holy Spirit. It's too hard for you to do on your own. Partner with God as He gives you the grace. But you do have to humble yourself and cry out to Him for help.

Jesus breathed on His disciples and said, "Receive the Holy Spirit!" (John 20:22 AMP). His next instruction was about forgiving people. Ask God to breathe the Holy Spirit onto you so that you can forgive those who've hurt you.

"Freely you have received, freely give" (Matthew 10:8 AMP). To forgive means "to excuse a fault, absolve from payment, pardon, send away, cancel, and bestow favor unconditionally." We are to do these things freely, from the heart.

Always remember the words of Proverbs 4:23 (ESV): "Keep your heart with all vigilance, for from it flow the springs of life."

The inspiring story of Corrie ten Boom has influenced millions of Christians for decades. She and her family hid Jews from the Nazis during World War II. They did this for years, until they were eventually discovered and they, too, were taken to a concentration camp. Corrie and her sister, Betsie, found themselves in Ravensbruck, one of the most notorious concentration camps, built to exterminate the Jews and their benefactors from the face of the earth. Betsie never left, dying a slow, agonizing, horrible death due to deprivation.

What did Corrie do with that heartbreak? After the end of World War II and her personal liberation, she left Holland to bring a message of forgiveness to Germany, home to the people who had enslaved her and stolen the life of her sister.

In 1947, after speaking to a small group at a church service in Munich, she glanced at the people departing and her breath was taken away. She immediately recognized a large man who nervously clutched a felt hat between his hands. He was one of the guards from the concentration camp. Corrie had just shared with the people: "When we confess our sins . . . God casts them into the deepest ocean, gone forever." Her words were too much for most people in that place and time to comprehend. But as people exited, one man, the guard, pushed his way forward. In a flash her mind went back to the concentration camp:

One moment I saw the overcoat and the brown hat; the next, a blue uniform and a visored cap with its skull and crossbones. It came back with a rush: the huge room with its harsh overhead lights; the pathetic pile of dresses and shoes in the center of the floor; the shame of walking naked past this man. I could see my sister's frail form ahead of me, ribs sharp beneath the parchment skin. Betsie, how thin you were!

When the guard thanked her for the message and agreed that our sins are at the bottom of the sea, Corrie froze. She fumbled with her purse. She didn't look him in the eyes. She couldn't take his outstretched hand. How could she? This man was responsible, in part, for the death of her sister and so many others.

When the man noted that she had spoken of her time in Ravensbruck, he admitted that he had been a guard there. All Corrie could see was the blue uniform and the leather crop swinging from his belt. All she wanted was to be away from this man. But he needed something from her—and perhaps he realized she needed something from him.

Looking her in the eyes he let her know that in his heart he knew God forgave him for his unspeakable cruelty and sins. But with tears he asked if he could hear it from her lips. Would she forgive him?

This was Corrie's moment of truth. Could she live what she was preaching? Could you or I under such circumstances?

And I stood there—I whose sins had every day to be forgiven—and could not [forgive]. Betsie had died in that place—could he erase her slow terrible death simply for the asking? . . .

And still I stood there with the coldness clutching my heart. But forgiveness is not an emotion—I knew that too. Forgiveness is an act of the will, and the will can function regardless of the temperature of the heart. "Jesus, help me!" I prayed silently. "I can lift my hand. I can do that much. You supply the feeling."

And so woodenly, mechanically, I thrust my hand into the one stretched out to me. And as I did, an incredible thing took place. The current started in my shoulder, raced down my arm, sprang into our joined hands. And then this healing warmth seemed to flood my whole being, bringing tears to my eyes.

"I forgive you, brother!" I cried. "With all my heart!"

For a long moment we grasped each other's hands, the former guard and the former prisoner. I had never known God's love so intensely, as I did then.[1]

Martin Luther King Jr. said, "He who is devoid of the power to forgive is also devoid of the power to love."[2]

We cannot give away what we haven't received. Thankfully, we have received the golden thread of mercy, of forgiveness, of love from our heavenly Father, and this allows us to pass on His forgiveness to others: "Once again you will have compassion on us. You will trample our sins under your feet, and throw them into the depths of the ocean" (Micah 7:19 NLT).

God's forgiveness toward us is radical and complete. It is part of the great mystery and victory of the cross. Yet until you fully receive God's grace and forgiveness, you'll never be able to fully forgive other people. I can truly say today that whatever was done to hurt me I have forgiven—in Jesus' name. And I can forgive only by the grace of God.

Did you know that sometimes the hardest person to forgive is yourself?

Maybe you've made decisions that have hurt others, and the thought of that brings you a lot of shame. Sometimes we have brought hurt intentionally, sometimes unintentionally. The whole process is painful to think about and can cause so much regret. I think as parents, we at some point have to say to our kids, "Oh, my, please forgive me. I really thought I knew what I was doing!" We need grace, grace, grace.

Ephesians 4 simply and lovingly says: "Get rid of all bitterness, rage and anger, brawling and slander, along with every form of malice. Be kind and compassionate to one another, forgiving each other, just as in Christ God forgave you" (vv. 31–32 NIV).

Just as Christ forgave you. Just as Christ forgave me. Forgive other people. The freedom that lies on the other side of forgiveness is not just life-changing, but life-saving, and it's not just for other people; it's for you as well. Receive His forgiveness today—the freedom on the other side of letting go is worth the leap.

10

WALKING IN
THE SPIRIT

*When we pray for the Spirit's help . . . we
will simply fall down at the Lord's feet in
our weakness. There we will find the victory
and power that comes from His love.*
—Andrew Murray, *Experiencing the Holy Spirit*

The Holy Spirit is a person, not an atmosphere. He creates an atmosphere, and He fills an atmosphere, but He is not *simply* an atmosphere. He is one person of a triune God. The Holy Spirit is always speaking and working on our behalf. He comes in power, and He works through the fruit of the Spirit in each of our lives. He operates with not just a *big bang* kind of power, but He also gives us the power to walk like Jesus walked—in the ways of love and forgiveness so that we can take the golden thread of God's love and mercy, the nature of His grace we have received in our own lives, and weave it into the lives of those around us. The Holy Spirit graces us with His power to live out His fruit:

> But the fruit of the Spirit is love, joy, peace, forbearance, kindness, goodness, faithfulness, and self-control. (Galatians 5:22–23 NIV)

In His prophetic nature, the Holy Spirit also prepares our hearts for what is to come. He is in fact preparing us all the time for what we are about to face. I find this fact about our Helper so comforting! I have seen this side of the Holy Spirit revealed in my own life in countless ways. One example is when I wrote the song "In Jesus' Name." I actually wrote it for a woman in our church who was battling cancer. Little did I know that the Holy Spirit was preparing my own heart for a battle that was soon to come. He gave me a song to sing over my own situation before I even knew about it.

In everything that He is and that He does, the Holy Spirit continues to reveal the incomparable love of the Father for His children on the earth.

> And hope does not put us to shame, because God's love has been poured out into our hearts through the Holy Spirit, who has been given to us. (Romans 5:5 NIV)

The love of God is what the golden thread is all about. Love is the very heart of the universe—and it has been since the time of its creation by its loving Creator. Love has always been and will always be—between the Father and the Son, between the Son and the Spirit, between the Spirit and the Father. Our triune God forms within Himself an unbreakable cord of Holy—all filled with the love of God. And this is the wonder of the saving grace of God that dwells within us—the holiness of grace that weaves its way throughout creation and through our world today by the power of the Spirit working within our lives.

One of the great fathers of the church, Saint Augustine, wrote the following words:

> Love, therefore, which is of God and is God, is specially the Holy Spirit, by whom the love of God is shed abroad in our hearts, by which love the whole Trinity dwells in us. And therefore most rightly is the Holy Spirit, although He is God, called also the gift of God. And by that gift what else can properly be understood except love, which brings to God, and without which any other gift of God whatsoever does not bring to God?[1]

The Holy Spirit is the One who opens our eyes and causes our awareness to increase—like wind and fire in our bones. The Hebrew word *ruach* means "blow" or "breath," and it refers to the wind of the Spirit blowing through our lives. The power of the Spirit ignites our lives with day-by-day, minute-by-minute, authentic lived-out worship of our amazing God, until we experience the growing and all-consuming flame of God's love being birthed in our spirits.

Another task of the Holy Spirit in our lives is to bring the Word of God to life in our circumstances and in our spirits. John 14:26 tells us that the Holy Spirit makes the Bible come alive for us. He gives us understanding into what the Scriptures speak into our situations—how we need to change, what steps we should take, how the Word needs to become *real* for us in our day-to-day lives.

To live in the fullness of God's sweet presence is His promise to us continually. But we need the Holy Spirit and the outworking of God's presence in our lives to see this come to fruition. To have the Holy Spirit as our advocate is to have God Himself indwelling us as believers. So, why in the world would we ever resist the working of the Holy Spirit in our lives? A man-made understanding of the Spirit and His outworkings in our lives has probably put more people off the Holy Spirit than anything else our enemy could throw at them.

We can resist the Holy Spirit by refusing to tune our ears and our hearts to His voice, especially if our hearts grow cold to the things of God due to hurts, disappointments, and bitterness. These things may start off small, cropping up in our relationships because of differences of opinion or for many other reasons, but they will result in a devastating root of bitterness taking hold in our lives. After I had encountered the Holy Spirit in my life, I felt Him start to disassemble the walls that I had built up around my heart. Uncomfortable? Very. Vital? Very.

HOLY SPIRIT, YOU ARE WELCOME HERE!

Maybe you've never been taught about the person of the Holy Spirit and the presence of God before. But if you start digging into the Word and looking back throughout your life, you will find that He's been walking with you and leading you all along. To put time aside to linger and wait to hear God's still, small voice is probably one of the hardest things for most of us to do. He can speak in the quiet; He can also speak in the chaos. I have learned that what I cultivate in the secret place is what I hear loud and clear as I go about life in the day to day.

When we trust in our own common sense or wisdom rather than in what the Holy Spirit is whispering to our hearts, then we can find ourselves resisting Him and His wisdom. And resisting Him can have devastating consequences for our lives and hearts and for the lives and hearts of the people on the earth today who need the presence of the Spirit to penetrate their world.

How do we resist Him?

We resist Him when the comfort of our flesh, or the pull of the status quo, trumps the conviction of following God with our entire being. We resist Him when condemnation, shame, and guilt block our ears to what the Holy Spirit is revealing to our hearts.

Don't allow this to happen in your life and in your heart!

Every morning wake up and yield your life over and over again, anew each and every day. When you get out of bed, let the first thing you say each morning be: "You are welcome here, Holy Spirit! Interrupt my day with Your voice!"

When He is invited into our lives, the Holy Spirit will take on the role of Guide and Counselor, leading us in the way we should go and revealing God's truth to us—both through His Word and in the everyday situations we encounter.

The Holy Spirit, in and through it all, will fill us continually with power to live and move and have our being *in Christ Jesus.* This is the purpose of His power in our lives and His speaking into our hearts. He speaks to us to make us more Christlike in every part of our lives, to sanctify us by His power, and He is speaking all the time! The problem is never whether He is speaking. The question is always, *Are we listening?*

RECOGNIZING THE SPIRIT'S VOICE

How can we recognize the Spirit's voice? How can we discern between our own thoughts and His leading? The Spirit of God lives within us. He not only teaches us how to pray, but the Holy Spirit is the Spirit of truth (John 14:16–17), and He leads us into all truth. He reminds us of Jesus' words, and He teaches us how to discern truth in this world today. He reveals God's will for our lives. Without the Person of the Holy Spirit living within us, we would not be able to discern the truth in any situation.

As we are learning to listen to the Holy Spirit, we must also learn to wait upon the Lord. Today there is a lot of talk about spiritual warfare, but I have come to believe that a large percentage of spiritual warfare consists of "waiting on the Lord." We often pray but receive no answers in our self-imposed time frame—not immediately. But often the gift is found in the waiting. And God is not intimidated by the time it takes.

I think there are times, when heaven seems silent and we find ourselves frustrated, that we take matters into our own hands. Like Sarah did with her maid, Hagar, trying to see if she could help God along with His promise to Abraham and her concerning a child. Staying in continual prayer teaches our hearts and minds to be open to the Holy Spirit's leading, but it also allows the Spirit to speak on our behalf:

> In the same way, the Spirit helps us in our weakness. We do not know what we ought to pray for, but the Spirit himself intercedes for us through wordless groans. And he who searches our hearts knows the mind of the Spirit, because the Spirit intercedes for God's people in accordance with the will of God. (Romans 8:26–27 NIV)

Be aware of the Holy Spirit's gentle tugging or pulling on your heart. You may not always understand what it means, but the peace of God will always accompany His true voice.

> And let the peace (soul harmony which comes) from Christ rule (act as umpire continually) in your hearts [deciding and settling with finality all questions that arise in your minds, in that peaceful state]. (Colossians 3:15 AMPC)

Not too long ago, I awakened early one morning with the strong desire to pray for a certain person. I have learned not to question whether or not God is speaking in these kinds of situations, but I am simply quick to say yes to the request and respond in faith to God's promptings. I found out later that in that *exact* moment, this person was in serious trouble and God had asked a bunch of us to pray. If I try to make sense of this on my own, it is too hard, but when I simply follow the gentle tug on my heart and obey, even if I may never know the outcome, my role is to just say *yes*.

Christ, the church's "head," does His work through His body, the church, many times by placing into our hearts certain words of warning and encouragement, burdens and assignments that He has for His people.

We are to be His vessels; He is the treasure that we, His vessels, hold!

The prophet Habakkuk said, "I will take my stand at my watchpost and station myself on the tower, and look out to see what he will say to me" (Habakkuk 2:1 ESV).

We know that prayer is not at all about informing God of things going on in which we could use His help, since He already knows about them anyway. Prayer is not about eloquence or knowledge, but in positioning ourselves to be ready for the answer in prayer, we also hear from God about what He wants to do in our lives, and by faith we lay hold of His provision for those things to take place.

There are things we will never understand while we are still in this world.

I have stepped out at times thinking I was following the Spirit's leading, and yet things did not work out as I felt they should have. But this is where my trust in my heavenly Father comes into view. I am learning to trust even when I am unsure of what is happening around me, even when what I think should happen doesn't. I believe God just loves it when we "have a go" at following Him. He can lead us easily when we are moving; just be open to His voice.

Among the last recorded words of Jesus on this earth are these:

"But you will receive power when the Holy Spirit comes on you; and you will be my witnesses in Jerusalem, and in all Judea and Samaria, and to the ends of the earth." (Acts 1:8 NIV)

Jesus lives *in you*—for you.

Jesus moves *on you*—for others.

In the book of Acts, the Word declares this treasured truth over our lives:

> "In the Last Days," God says,
> "I will pour out my Spirit
>   on every kind of people:
> Your sons will prophesy,
>   also your daughters;
> Your young men will see visions,
>   your old men dream dreams.
> When the time comes,
>   I'll pour out my Spirit
> On those who serve me, men and women both,
>   and they'll prophesy.
> I'll set wonders in the sky above
>   and signs on the earth below,
> Blood and fire and billowing smoke,
>   the sun turning black and the moon blood-red,
> Before the Day of the Lord arrives,
>   the Day tremendous and marvelous;
> And whoever calls out for help
>   to me, God, will be saved."
>
>   (ACTS 2:17–21 THE MESSAGE)

The Holy Spirit has always come in power, and God's Spirit is being poured out on His people in this very day upon the earth.

When we open our hearts to Jesus, we begin a journey in Christ toward regeneration. We are transformed by God's love and made alive by His Spirit. The old becomes new and our true identity in Him is brought to life. This is the regeneration of the Spirit life in which we are now walking, the power of God's Spirit in our lives.

In Christ, our identity is defined, not by what we do, but by whose we are. John 13:35 says that we are to be known by our love for one another, the golden thread of mercy that is a pure reflection of the Father God spilling out from our lives into the lives of those around us.

In John 3, Jesus taught one of the religious leaders of His day about the importance of the conversion experience and the indwelling of the Holy Spirit:

> Now there was a man of the Pharisees, named Nicodemus, a ruler of the Jews; this man came to Jesus by night and said to Him, "Rabbi, we know that You have come from God as a teacher; for no one can do these signs that You do unless God is with him." Jesus answered and said to him, "Truly, truly, I say to you, unless one is born again he cannot see the kingdom of God."
>
> Nicodemus said to Him, "How can a man be born when he is old? He cannot enter a second time into his mother's womb and be born, can he?" Jesus answered, "Truly, truly, I say to you, unless one is born of water and the Spirit he cannot enter into the kingdom of God. That which is born of the flesh is flesh, and that which is born of the Spirit is spirit. Do not be amazed that I said to you, 'You must be born again.' The wind blows where it wishes and you hear the sound of it, but do not know where it comes from and where it is going; so is everyone who is born of the Spirit." (John 3:1–8 NASB)

This passage of Scripture leads powerfully into the most famous of Jesus' statements:

> For God so loved the world, that He gave His only begotten Son, that whoever believes in Him shall not perish, but have eternal life. (John 3:16 NASB)

The primary work of God's presence through the power of the Holy Spirit is to empower us to be witnesses to the saving grace of Jesus Christ. The Holy Spirit is always revealing the love of the Father to all mankind on the earth. Jesus said:

> "For John baptized with water, but you will be baptized with the Holy Spirit not many days from now."
>
> So when they had come together, they were asking Him, saying, "Lord, is it at this time You are restoring the kingdom to Israel?" He said to them, "It is not for you to know times or epochs which the Father has fixed by His own authority; but you will receive power when the Holy Spirit has come upon you; and you shall be My witnesses both in Jerusalem, and in all Judea and Samaria, and even to the remotest part of the earth." (Acts 1:5–8 NASB)

And so, my dear friends, we are to live our whole lives as living witnesses—energized and fueled by the limitless Person of the Holy Spirit, both knowing Him and bearing His fruit and His power and authority. Holy Spirit power brings into our lives great boldness, transforming energy, gentleness when needed, a love for others like you have never known, as well as the authority to pray so that evil will flee our lives and our world. And as we practice the presence of God in our lives more and more each day, we grow to be more and more like Jesus, and the golden thread weaves its way through our lives in greater and more purposeful ways.

I pray we continue to stay aware of the Spirit's work and whispers in our hearts and minds. Let us stay ever mindful of His workings and will, and let us continually, day by day, moment by moment, breath by breath, invite Him into our world.

Welcome, Holy Spirit! Have Your way in me!

11

HOLY DISCONTENT

The best thing is to flee from the all to the All.
—Teresa of Avila, *The Way of Perfection*

One of the reasons I fell in love with my husband, Checkie, was his heart for others. As a youth leader he was kind and compassionate, as a leader of the band we were both playing in he was fair, fun, and always looking out for everyone's best interests. But I actually loved the way he honored my mum, who by then was a single mum working extra hard to help provide the best for her kids. He would take her flowers from his own garden as a little way of bringing honor to a woman who was doing her best in a season that was tougher than I will ever really understand.

As love pulled Mark's and my lives together, so did purpose, as I watched him work out some of the things his heart had become restless over, while I was more self-conscious and needed encouragement to step out and do what my heart was telling me to do. I am not sure whether I was being overly cautious, whether I was being too polite, whether my confidence was not at a place to even think I could be an answer to someone else's need, or whether it was just my foolish pride that would keep me from responding in the way I knew deep down that I wanted to.

But in the midst of falling in love, God was also bringing two very different people together to complement each other, to challenge each other, and to accomplish far more than we ever could have accomplished on our own. Mark has always been a pioneer, and he has always been an incredibly inspiring visionary. And I guess because of my upbringing, I had this idea that I would get married young, settle down, raise a love-filled family, love and serve God simply and purely, sing a little here and there, and gather all my chickadees around me. I would always be calm and comfortable, I would create a home that would be a refuge—you get the picture. But God has had His grip on our hearts for a long time, and this has required me to be comfortable with being uncomfortable, to have an open hand with all the things He has given us to steward.

As human beings, we naturally tend to do whatever we can to minimize being uncomfortable. People love to keep things "just so," and many love the comfort of pain-free living. I know I do. But how easily we can flatten our emotional lives down to the level of our being okay with a "beige" existence. And as the earth continues to heave with fear and people are grappling for hope that is greater than their anxiety, we all need to become more comfortable with being uncomfortable. I've spoken before about the discomfort of living with a new heart, as we can see in this passage where God says:

> And I will give them one heart, and put a new spirit within them. And I will take the heart of stone out of their flesh and give them a heart of flesh, that they may walk in My statutes

and keep My ordinances and do them. Then they will be My people, and I shall be their God. (Ezekiel 11:19–20 NASB)

NOT ON MY WATCH!

Yes, our new hearts sure do ask us to step out of ourselves—again and again. This is what happens to our hearts when we become Christ-followers. As we are made more and more into God's image, we live with a tension that does not leave room for a beige existence.

When I read through the Scriptures, I find many godly men and women who at some point found something they just could not accept as being okay. They would stand up, often risking their lives, or they would willingly lay down their lives, in order to see things made right. This was their "Not on my watch!" moment.

Esther had a choice to make when she realized she had been given the opportunity to stand up and speak for the freedom of her people. Or she could have chosen to just continue to live comfortably within the palace, looking after herself and enjoying all the luxuries surrounding her. She could have excused herself from the trauma unfolding outside the palace walls. Instead she risked her reputation and even death to do what she knew to be right. You know the rest of the story:

> Then Mordecai told them to reply to Esther, "Do not imagine that you in the king's palace can escape any more than all the Jews. For if you remain silent at this time, relief and deliverance will arise for the Jews from another place and you and your father's house will perish. And who knows whether you have not attained royalty for such a time as this?" (Esther 4:13–14 NASB)

To this challenge, Esther said yes. She risked it all, played her part, and saved her people. *Not on my watch!*

Nehemiah is another person mentioned in the Bible who declared, "Not on my watch!" The Israelite people were vulnerable. The city walls were broken down, and their enemies were laughing out loud and making a mockery of the God of the Israelites. Nehemiah took a leave of absence from his office as a cupbearer to the king. He prayed, prepared himself, and then began to restore the city walls and reconstruct the temple to keep his nation safe. He could not stand the situation anymore, and so he did something about it.

Nehemiah's enemies failed, because "God had brought their plot to nothing" (Nehemiah 4:15 NKJV). God used the opposition of Judah's enemies to drive His people to their knees. Prayer works! And not surprisingly, Nehemiah gave all the glory to God as his plans succeeded, saying, "My God put it into my heart" (7:5 NKJV). It was God who accomplished the goal. Nehemiah was humble and trusting, and yet he was so discontented with the way things were that he stepped out in faith, trusted God's leadership, and made a way for the vulnerable people. He had made the decision to say, "Not on my watch!"

Even as a shepherd boy, David had learned that some things just couldn't happen on his watch!

> Goliath stood and shouted to the ranks of Israel, "Why do you come out and line up for battle? Am I not a Philistine, and are you not the servants of Saul? Choose a man and have him come down to me. If he is able to fight and kill me, we will become your subjects; but if I overcome him and kill him, you will become our subjects and serve us." Then the Philistine said, "This day I defy the armies of Israel! Give me a man and

let us fight each other." On hearing the Philistine's words, Saul and all the Israelites were dismayed and terrified. (1 Samuel 17:8–11 NIV)

Goliath stood and mocked David's God and His precious people. Yet even as a young man, David said no to this kind of behavior. What a story!

David said to Saul, "Let no one lose heart on account of this Philistine; your servant will go and fight him."

Saul replied, "You are not able to go out against this Philistine and fight him; you are only a young man, and he has been a warrior from his youth."

But David said to Saul, "Your servant has been keeping his father's sheep. When a lion or a bear came and carried off a sheep from the flock, I went after it, struck it and rescued the sheep from its mouth. When it turned on me, I seized it by its hair, struck it and killed it. Your servant has killed both the lion and the bear; this uncircumcised Philistine will be like one of them, because he has defied the armies of the living God. The LORD who rescued me from the paw of the lion and the paw of the bear will rescue me from the hand of this Philistine."

Saul said to David, "Go, and the LORD be with you."

Then Saul dressed David in his own tunic. He put a coat of armor on him and a bronze helmet on his head. David fastened on his sword over the tunic and tried walking around, because he was not used to them.

"I cannot go in these," he said to Saul, "because I am not used to them." So he took them off. Then he took his staff in his hand, chose five smooth stones from the stream, put them in the pouch of his shepherd's bag and, with his sling in his hand, approached the Philistine. . . .

David said to the Philistine, "You come against me with

sword and spear and javelin, but I come against you in the name of the LORD Almighty, the God of the armies of Israel, whom you have defied. . . ."

So David triumphed over the Philistine with a sling and a stone; without a sword in his hand he struck down the Philistine and killed him.

David ran and stood over him. He took hold of the Philistine's sword and drew it from the sheath. After he killed him, he cut off his head with the sword. (1 Samuel 17:32–40, 45, 50–51 NIV)

With God on his side and a fire in his belly to put wrong things right, David defeated the enemy. David was courageous and trusting, young and inexperienced. Yet he was filled with a passionate sense of justice, and also, may I add, he was not happy to go out in someone else's strength or anointing. In the name of the Lord, he took what he had in his hand, and he defeated the enemy.

FIND YOUR PLACE TO TAKE A STAND

When you feel something rising within you, a holy discontent, an unwillingness to settle for unjust circumstances, this will give you a clue as to your purpose in life. I watched this holy discontent rise and gather momentum in my husband's life, and over the years he has stood in the gap for so many people. His personal "not on my watch" moments have been walked out over the days, months, and years of his life, right up to the point where we are now leading a church together. Mark has stood and taken his place, following a God moment that would not let him go—and here we are today.

The stirrings we feel in our spirits, the situations that frustrate us—we must always listen to them closely, as they often highlight the things we were born to make right, not just allow to fly by. As Christ-followers, born and made in the image of God, we *will* encounter things that make us feel a holy sense of discontent. These are our personal "not on my watch" moments.

Sometimes we are waiting for big moments to bring our sense of resolve, when I have found that God is actually just asking us to tend to the mostly unseen and quietly evil practices that are everywhere around us, if we would open the eyes of our hearts to actually see them.

The "holy discontent" that is intricately woven within each of us can be buried under what the experts call "problem fatigue," which occurs when we start to think that a certain problem is too big for us to handle or have any effect on. But we were not born to live and die and simply be happy with our lot in life. Remember the words of Isaiah 61: "The Spirit of the LORD is upon me *because* . . ." He has called us to make a difference in this world!

Like many of you reading this book, I've always been moved by people who are hurting. It does not bring indifference to my heart; it brings a fire to my belly to bring change wherever I see that I can. I am sure that many of you feel the same way. But not everything you put your hand to needs to have an organization born out of it; many times, it is just the way of love leading us to small and yet powerful moments of standing in the gap and speaking up for others wherever we can. After my bout with cancer, I have felt so much braver to speak to people I see on the street, or wherever I am, who are hurting. This has been one of the greatest gifts cancer has given me.

People need to know they are seen. And when you know and understand the freedom and hope that Jesus brings, you will be filled with a renewed passion to make sure that everyone has the opportunity to know Christ. Whether we are living in dire circumstances or living in excess, people are people, and we *all* need the love of God. As I speak to strangers, I don't often start by talking about Jesus. I just go out in the power of His love. I find that most people are open to a genuine conversation. I might start by telling them that I felt prompted to come over and say hi. I share my story, and I listen to theirs. It may not be changing a nation, but for one person, I am bringing hope into their world. Even if I appear foolish to them, the gift of getting older is that I don't really mind.

It's all about taking the love of Jesus and His power everywhere we go. It is not about the things we cannot do; it's about walking in the moments that God gives us, allowing the miraculous to work in our lives as we tend to whatever God puts in our hands. Many times I don't even get to see the results of the things that I start, but my commitment is simply to be obedient to God's purposes for my life.

Sometimes you will be a part of bringing change that is about culture, or church health, or prayer. I'll never forget many years ago the elders of a church telling me that if I brought a keyboard into the church, I would not be welcomed back. (Electric keyboards were too "of this world" for them.) I could not do much at that time. I was just eighteen years old and had little experience and no authority. But with a fire in my belly and the grace of God to be calm and loving in a new space of worship, I've been able to, many years later, join with the great gathering of leaders of worship around the earth. Together we've been able to see music do what it was meant to do, which is not for believers to just sing songs in church, but for every man, woman, and child to engage in the great eternal anthem of worship that rises from our hearts to His, by His grace and for His glory, welcoming the Holy Spirit in power and might as the atmosphere morphs to the sound of heaven on earth. Oh, what a divine privilege!

David had a slingshot, a stone, and the power of God. Esther had a godly uncle, a crown, and a voice. Nehemiah had favor with the king, a heart that burned for the Lord's people, and a fire in his belly to bring about change. At some point, all of them had to take a deep breath and say *yes* to the unknown, following their holy discontent. God had a planet full of people who needed a way to Him, and He had a Son who was willing to lay down His life for us, who in the end said yes: "Not My will, but Yours be done."

WHAT IS YOUR HOLY DISCONTENT?

And so, with that in mind, let me ask you the big question: What is *your* holy discontent?

Perhaps it's something personal.

Perhaps it's something in your family.

Is it a need in the community that breaks your heart but which you feel helpless to change?

Some dear girlfriends in our church family and myself started the "1,000 meal project." While walking through my cancer treatments, I saw so many families in our community who were taking this same journey with very little practical support. Being part of a church family meant that my own family was never without meals and love during my own tough time, but I met so many others who were just out there on their own. I could not stand the idea that people had to walk through this evil illness without a greater community to walk with them. So now people in our local community can just send us an e-mail, and we will provide meals for these families at no charge—and with those meals come people who walk in a whole lot of love.

I was so weak during my own cancer treatments and unable to do much, but I had a whole lot of girlfriends in my church who knew how to cook and who loved to be part of the answer. They modeled an unspeakable beauty and love to my family during that time and set a godly example for us to follow through on for others.

One of the greatest current-day stories of someone who stood up for the plight of others is that of Malala Yousafzai. Her powerful speech, given as she was awarded the Nobel Peace Prize, is simply inspiring:

> Thousands of people have been killed by the terrorists and millions have been injured. I am just one of them.
>
> So here I stand . . . One girl among many.
>
> I speak—not for myself, but for all girls and boys.
>
> I raise up my voice—not so that I can shout, but so that those without a voice can be heard. . . .
>
> The Taliban thought that the bullets would silence us. But they failed. And then, out of that silence, came thousands of voices. The terrorists thought that they would change our aims and stop our ambitions, but nothing changed in my life except this: Weakness, fear, and hopelessness died. Strength, power, and courage were born. I am the same Malala. My ambitions are the same. My hopes are the same. My dreams are the same.[1]

Oh, my! Talk about using your own personal tragedy to help others walking through similar terrifying ordeals. This girl became an instant legend. This was her "not on my watch" moment.

When I continue to think about God's holy discontent, I realize that His agenda was not driven by opinion, but it was driven by *love*. His "not on my watch" moment was what ultimately happened on the cross, as He died for you and for me.

My challenge to all of us today is that whatever your holy discontent is—*feed it!* The temptation is to avoid it, to stay away from it, or to ignore it, because in some ways it would be easier. But I say, even if others try to dissuade you, get on top of that thing that truly stirs your heart.

Life is *not* about being comfortable. Life is about *purpose.* We would have a lot less unhappy people on this earth if they went out in search of purpose rather than comfort.

In this season of your life, why don't you take the time to get quiet before God and ask Him the question: *What is my life here on earth for?* We are all here for a purpose, and it's exciting to discover what it is that we can apply ourselves to in order to see freedom brought to the hurting people of this world.

Psalm 18:2 tells us, "The LORD is my protector, he is my strong fortress. My God is my protection, and with him I am safe. He protects me like a shield; he defends me and keeps me safe" (GNT).

The more I step out in response to need, the easier it becomes. It's good to remember on the journey, however, that people are not projects to be fixed, but simply people to be loved, people who are on a journey just like we are. I have so many friends who are doing amazing things on the coast of Australia and beyond as they have responded to their own holy discontent. Whether it be addressing homelessness or domestic violence, or building HIV-AIDS hospitals, or forming homework clubs for kids, or promoting chaplaincy in schools, or simply reaching out to a lonely neighbor, there are always tasks entrusted to us.

Jesus modeled a life in which He was willing to stop everything when He encountered a moment when He could tend to someone's need, and His example gives us a beautiful image of the power of someone being seen, and known, and cared for.

A few years ago, I had the privilege of traveling to Calcutta and going to the places where Mother Teresa lived out her calling, fueled by her holy discontent. She slept in the most humble of small rooms, but she lived with such intentionality that, history tells us, even powerful men of government would cower when she walked into a room, as she was a woman on a mission, doing all she could to ensure that people could die with dignity.

> "For I was hungry and you gave me something to eat, I was thirsty and you gave me something to drink, I was a stranger and you invited me in, I needed clothes and you clothed me, I was sick and you looked after me, I was in prison and you came to visit me."
>
> Then the righteous will answer him, "Lord, when did we see you hungry and feed you, or thirsty and give you something to drink? When did we see you a stranger and invite you in, or needing clothes and clothe you? When did we see you sick or in prison and go to visit you?"
>
> The King will reply, "Truly I tell you, whatever you did for one of the least of these brothers and sisters of mine, you did for me." (Matthew 25:35–40 NIV)

Whatever you feel God is speaking to your heart about, why don't you start just doing what you can do to help bring about a resolve? Talk to your pastors and your friends. But don't be a lone ranger and get all out of sorts when not everyone gets behind *your* holy discontent. God is big, and the Holy Spirit is able to take what little you have and use it for His glory. When God beckons you, move forward, and when you hear Him speak, *respond!* His plans are not to harm you, but rather they are always filled with *hope* eternal! Grab your slingshot—let's do this thing!

ONE WITH HIM

But the person who is joined to the
Lord is one spirit with him.
—1 CORINTHIANS 6:17 NLT

OCEAN WAVES CRASHING ON THE SHORELINE. A SALTY BREEZE tousling your hair. Seagulls circling lazily overhead. When you feel the sand of the beach under your feet and the sound of the ocean crashing onto the shore, your nervous system immediately calms down. Your worries melt away as you connect with God's creation all around you, and with the Creator Himself as He restores your soul.

At times as I sit peacefully on the shore, it is like I can literally feel creation praising God all around me, and my soul finds its own song of solace and strength. I simply cannot run into my day without breathing deeply and thanking God for every moment He has given me, and then listening to the sweet Holy Spirit as I find a healthy order for my day. I used to be able to grab my "God fix" as I ran out the door, which I am sure He is fine with, but there is so much more to be received as we take time in this two-way relationship.

A part of me is such a hard worker, and through many seasons of searching to find my identity in the work that I have achieved, the necessity of rest eluded me. Somehow I always felt as if I would be letting others down if I took any time out for myself to refuel. I am not entirely sure where these thoughts of mine originated, but maybe being the eldest child, working full-time from a very young age, caused me to view work as my go-to filler of my time—and I have got to add that I have mostly enjoyed it that way!

But living like this for years, not finding enough space to draw many deep breaths in a row, I found myself in a state of great harm to my soul and my physical body. It wasn't until that cancer diagnosis that I finally learned to take the idea of rest seriously. When first they told me that I would be in treatment for twelve months, and that I needed to give myself to that time frame in my body *and* in my mind—oh, the wrestle and the struggle and the frustration— that is something I cannot find words for.

And then, when they said it would take an additional few *years* for me to find my "new normal"—let's just say, I didn't greet the news with joy and elation. My heart, my soul, and my mind were all at odds with one another, and I was a jumbled mess of grief, fear, guilt, and annoyance. Of course, I was so very thankful that I was still alive, but my internal conflict was real and it tested me beyond what I thought I could handle. Purely through the grace of God, that golden thread of hope and love and mercy found its way to my inner man—Him loving me, holding me safely, and hiding me in Him throughout the entire process.

Still, the sacred rest that the entirety of my being was craving was suddenly required of me—it was no longer optional! It was put upon me like an ill-fitting jacket, and I had to learn to allow that jacket to fit itself to my body and my life.

Somehow, as I now felt quite useless *and* a burden to many of the people around me, especially to my family, I wasn't at all sure how the calling of God would work anymore. I was in a forced season of not just sitting down—but literally lying flat on my back, at times feeling like I was not going to make it through the day, unable to function in my favorite roles as wife, mum, and grammie.

Being awakened to the sense of a spiritual calling or divine purpose on my life as a newly saved teenager wasn't hard. In fact, it was so strong initially that, because of my lack of self-esteem, my innate response was at first to run. I acted a little bit like Jonah; although I don't love the smell of seafood, I cannot even comprehend the whole belly-of-the-whale experience! But it wasn't long before our youth group leaders, and the music ministry leaders at my church, pulled me close and began to love me just as I was. They helped me to learn about the things of God, the Word of God, and His purposes, and this is where not only the holiness of church community truly came to be so precious in my life, but also where I learned to feel the glory of God's presence with me as He aligned me to His plans for my life.

It's interesting to me that I cannot remember a season when I wasn't treated as a leader. There were never any hoops presented for me to jump through. There have been very few times I can remember that being a woman in leadership was even an issue. Instead, I was given a whole lot of patience, grace, and love from a whole lot of people—a community of faith and of friends who became family to me.

Some of the friends I made in that season are still dear friends to me today. As we hungered after the presence and power of God as young "green teens," those experiences knit our hearts together for life.

As the Bible tells us in the Song of Songs:

> The one I love calls to me:
> "Arise, my dearest. Hurry, my darling.
> Come away with me!
> I have come as you have asked

to draw you to my heart and lead you out.
For now is the time, my beautiful one.
The season has changed,
the bondage of your barren winter has ended,
and the season of hiding is over and gone.
The rains have soaked the earth
and left it bright with blossoming flowers.
The season for singing and pruning the vines has arrived.
I hear the cooing of doves in our land,
filling the air with songs to awaken you
and guide you forth.
Can you not discern this new day of destiny
breaking forth around you?
The early signs of my purposes and plans
are bursting forth.
The budding vines of new life
are now blooming everywhere.
The fragrance of their flowers whispers,
'There is change in the air.'"

(SONG OF SONGS 2:10–13 TPT)

The glory of God and His eternal kindness is so much grander than I ever knew before, and so much lovelier and more personal than my desire to please Him and "work for Him" could ever be. To know that the One I love is truly satisfied with me fills my spirit with joy. He has spoken to my heart in ways that have reframed my mind. I know deeply that even if I did not do one more thing *for* Him, He still would call me His beloved, and He purely and wholeheartedly desires that my heart would rest in Him.

Now, there are many things in life that will not be achieved without hard work. Each of us will encounter many necessary seasons of building and pioneering in our lives. We all must learn the satisfaction that comes from hard work and actually achieving or creating something, and the joy that accompanies the rhythm of work as the "sweet hum of momentum" brings a consistency to our accomplishments. But from my perspective now, after having been through quite a few seasons of life already, I would love to be able to sit down with my younger self and say, "Sweet girl, the key to sustaining the *real* riches in this life is learning to *be*, learning to simply *receive* the gift of God's love, and learning to *know* who you are in Christ!"

For each of us, our identity cries out for meaning, because each one of us has been designed for purpose. And yes, we are so much more than what we do, but still it is often hard to separate who we are from what we do, because as we walk out our lives on purpose, and *in* our purpose, the glory of God is revealed in such beautiful and powerful ways. But just because one season may be changing does not mean that your entire story is over. Your story is still unfolding, and the choices you make today about how to nourish your soul will greatly affect your future!

Often in seasons of transition, we tend to forget who we are. We forget that sense of knowing our purpose, and at times our value, and unfortunately this makes the transitions in our lives that much more difficult as we wrestle with the age-old sin of self. During this time of healing and reflection, Mark and I decided that we would keep the key things in our world—that we could control—consistent and central. Church, family dinners, work and school routines, exercise, healthy food, time spent in the Word—these things became the bedrock of our daily routine, and for us and our kids, every day these little continuities became an important part of our soul health. They kept our eyes on the seemingly insignificant little joy-filled milestones rather than on the fear that nipped at our heels.

Dear friend, in whatever season you find yourself, identify your little daily sacred spaces, and please be sure to take the time that you need to breathe, to think, to pray, to listen—to simply *be*. Sometimes we need to be standing at attention, activated, ready at our post, down in the trenches with others, doing the things we know that we *can* do—but there are also times when we need to remember that we are just as valuable *while we are seated*. Sometimes we simply need to be seated at God's table of plenty as He restores our souls.

This is described so beautifully in Psalm 23. The glory of God displayed in my life is just as powerful in any season, because His glory is not yours or mine to adjust or tamper with. God's goodness is not diminished whether I am standing or sitting. No, His goodness is His goodness, just because He is God and He is good, not based on anything I accomplish or do not accomplish.

THE VALUE OF COMMUNITY

In addition, maybe we all need to remember that the church is not a place *where we go*; it's a part of *who we are*. We are Christ's body. The word *busybody* doesn't sound very attractive—and that's because it isn't. Our purpose is to be known by our love, which we can show purely by the power of God's love at work in us. And we walk this out in *any* season. Over the years, I've seen a lot of people grow tired of the church or become disappointed or frustrated with their own sense of belonging. Maybe the church has been confusing the meaning of service and servants, but because of that confusion, people have been walking away from not just the church but sometimes even the faith, and most often from the purposes of God for their lives.

When we become out of sorts with God's church, when we disregard His body, we miss out on *so* much that God has promised us if we yield our lives here on earth to His purposes. And His purposes are most often carved out within the context of community.

Only let your manner of life be worthy of the gospel of Christ, so that whether I come and see you or am absent, I may hear of you that you are standing firm in one spirit, with one mind striving side by side for the faith of the gospel, and not frightened in anything by your opponents. This is a clear sign to them of their destruction, but of your salvation, and that from God. (Philippians 1:27–28 ESV)

It is only in the context of community that we grow in our understanding of Christ's body, God's kingdom, and the fulfillment of His plans for our lives. We were never designed to do life alone. We were designed for relationship—with our triune God and with each other.

We need each other! When you are at a low point, you need me to come alongside you and walk with you while you find your strength again. When I am weak, I need you to walk with me, to pray with me, to encourage me. This is the meaning of the body of Christ. You play your part, designed for you. I play my part, designed for me. There is room for all of us, but there is *no* room for us to compete. That is a waste of precious emotion and resources, and it will eventually gnaw away at the beauty of the journey that we are meant to experience together.

DOES YOUR LIFE MATTER?

So, does it really matter? Does my small part in the mystery of God's purposes really matter? If we are called "important and valuable" to God, but also "dust," does any of it even really matter?

Yes, my friend! Your life matters very much. And God's purpose for your life matters very much. As we walk in Christ, rest in Christ, and grow in Christ, we will grow in confidence as to what He has called us to do. Our job is to be at rest while we walk out each day expecting His leading to be upon our lives. Keep alert! He is speaking and leading all the time.

The purposes of a person's heart are deep waters, but one who
has insight draws them out. (Proverbs 20:5 NIV)

I sat down with Mark not long ago and marveled at how the
Lord has led us and given us faith and courage to keep taking steps
toward where He is leading. We were reminded how one day, as I
was stressing about finding God's will, a visiting minister came to
our church, pointed to me, and said, "The Lord hears you and He
says, 'Daughter, if you go to the right, I will bless you, and if you go
to the left, I will bless you.'"

Immediately I felt the strain leave me as I realized that God
was simply asking me to step out where I felt was right, and He
would lead me and direct my steps. I think that if we just get on
with loving God and others, it's pretty hard to get out of His will.
God is always working to fulfill His purposes. He is just looking
for willing vessels!

Therefore, my dear friends, as you have always obeyed—not only
in my presence, but now much more in my absence—continue
to work out your salvation with fear and trembling, for it is God
who works in you to will and to act in order to fulfill his good
purpose. (Philippians 2:12–13 NIV)

Throughout your lifetime, you will be offered wonderful
opportunities that maybe don't feel quite right. It's crazy how
often we talk ourselves into something we know isn't right, just to
please others, even when we know that it's not really God's best for
our lives. Can I encourage you to take the time you need to hear
from the Lord and then be brave in your decision to wait for God's
best? This may mean that you need to walk away from seemingly
"good things." And what you are doing may look foolish to some,
but I guarantee, in God's economy you will never miss out. There's
so much to be learned and so much joy to be experienced when

you sense the indescribable "yes and amen!" in your spirit regarding God's true purpose for you.

Pastor Rick Warren wrote:

> You were planned for God's pleasure. The moment you were born into the world, God was there as an unseen witness, *smiling* at your birth. He wanted you alive, and your arrival gave him great pleasure. God did not *need* to create you, but he *chose* to create you for his own enjoyment. You exist for his benefit, his glory, his purpose and his delight.[1]

The Bible says, "Because of his love God had already decided that through Jesus Christ he would make us his children—this was his pleasure and purpose" (Ephesians 1:4–5 GNT).

Striving. Competing. Self-loathing. Busyness. Feeling maxed out. Feeling stressed. These words describe how many people exist today, yet the Lord is saying to His beloved people, "Come and let Me quench your thirst. Come and be with Me, so that I can fill you, lead you, and guide you into all truth! Just come to Me. Allow Me to walk with you right into the middle of your purpose, the very thing I have designed you to accomplish and to be in this world."

John Piper has said, "God is most glorified in us when we are most satisfied in Him."[2] And Saint Irenaeus of Lyons said, "The glory of God is man fully alive."[3] Are you fully alive today? Are you striving or resting? Yield to Him. Unite your heart with His, and make His will your own. You won't regret it for one moment.

Settle in to Him.

Enter into His rest.

Breathe in His Spirit and experience His peace.

13

HIS STRENGTH, MY COURAGE

Where God guides, God provides.
—FRANK N. D. BUCHMAN, *REMAKING THE WORLD*

AFTER WE MOVED TO THE CENTRAL COAST OF NEW SOUTH Wales, Australia, I decided to check out our new local shopping center. It was a rather memorable shopping trip, as I was asked by three separate people (all strangers to me) during that one outing whether they could pray with me or prophesy over me. The whole experience was so very lovely and natural, albeit a little intense, and I went home thinking that Jesus must have moved to Erina Fair!

As I walked into a homewares store, a beautiful girl who worked there said, "I have asked my pastor that if ever I saw you here, could I please give you this word that I feel is for you. I see and hear thousands of regal horses galloping up the freeway toward the Central Coast. This picture represents strength and leadership, literally galloping together in response to the many prayers that have been prayed over this region for many, many years. God has said that you are here as a part of this prophesy."

You can imagine how this made me feel! I hugged her and thanked her, then grabbed my groceries and an extra-large latte and headed home. I have pondered that word from the Lord so many times. I have even been awakened by its powerful imagery, the sound of galloping horses' hooves en masse running up the freeway. I found a soundbite of galloping horses and played it to the women of our church family, and we prayed over what this could possibly look like into the future. Every time I think of it, it's like a little fire burns deeper in my spirit, refining me and my family to being right where God wants us to be.

After I received that word, I began to study the concept of horses in the Old and New Testaments. I found that horses represent strength—and in the realm of the Spirit, horses can also signify war, for an army's strength was often evaluated by the amount and type of literal horsepower the army had at its disposal. Many images come to mind, including the sheer strength of horsepower uniting in common purpose.

Over and over, the Spirit of God impressed upon me that His heart for our region would never be accomplished by "strength in ourselves," as the psalms remind us. Many people trust in chariots or in horses—but that is not what we are to do. We are to trust in the name of our God.

The horse, however, also represents a regal beauty with its shiny coat, strong legs, and determined spirit. Horses have the thunderous ability to gain speed and momentum as they move into a gallop—both literally and figuratively. And then the Spirit of God took me to Esther 8. Let's take a look at this account in this particular context. We will be picking up the story *after* Esther has been used mightily by God. The new queen had risked her whole self—everything she had, including her own life—for the purpose of saving her people. And yet she trusted in God to deliver them all—and He did, in a miraculous way.

The enemy of the Jews at that time, Haman, was ultimately destroyed, hanged on the gallows he had prepared for the innocent Mordecai, Esther's uncle. King Ahasuerus gave Esther all Haman's property, which she promptly handed over to Mordecai, who had walked with her throughout the whole challenge.

Esther then asked the king if he would reverse Haman's written proposal to destroy the Jewish people. She could not stand by and watch her people plundered and slaughtered when it was within her power to stop it. The king asked Mordecai to rewrite the law concerning the Jews and to seal it with his signet ring. Mordecai was then to provide this script announcing the Jewish freedom to every province—in their own language so that it would be easily understood.

> He wrote [a decree] in the name of King Ahasuerus, and sealed it with the king's ring, and sent letters by couriers on horseback, riding on the royal [mail] relay horses, the offspring of the racing mares. In it the king granted the Jews who were in every city the right to assemble and to defend their lives; to destroy, to kill, and to annihilate any armed force that might attack them, their little children, and women; and to take the enemies' goods as plunder, on one day in all the provinces of King Ahasuerus, the thirteenth [day] of the twelfth month (that is, the month of Adar). A copy of the edict was to be issued as a law in every province and as a proclamation to all peoples, so that the Jews would be ready on that day, to avenge themselves on their enemies. So the couriers, who were mounted on the royal relay horses, left quickly, urged on by the king's command; and the decree was issued at the citadel in Susa [the capital].

Then Mordecai departed from the presence of the king in royal apparel of blue and white, with a large crown of gold and with a robe of fine linen and purple wool; and the city of Susa shouted and rejoiced. For [at this time] the Jews had light [a dawn of new hope] and gladness and joy and honor. In each and every province and in each and every city, wherever the king's command and his decree arrived, the Jews celebrated with gladness and joy, a feast and a holiday. And many among the peoples of the land became Jews, for the fear of the Jews [and their God] had fallen on them. (Esther 8:10–17 AMP)

The royal decree was announced by sending a message via the royal horses, a message that declared ultimate victory and safety, that shouted out to all that the Lord had brought forth a new light—the dawn of a new hope! It was just as He promised would take place in Isaiah 42:9: "Everything I prophesied has come true, and now I will prophesy again. I will tell you the future before it happens" (NLT).

> Lift up your eyes and look about you:
> All assemble and come to you;
> your sons come from afar,
> and your daughters are carried on the hip.
> Then you will look and be radiant,
> your heart will throb and swell with joy;
> the wealth on the seas will be brought to you,
> to you the riches of the nations will come.
>
> (ISAIAH 60:4–5 NIV)

Close your eyes and hear the sound of horses' hooves galloping against the ground, of the mighty horses thundering across the plains. They do not just represent the strength of the Lord for us; they also represent the carriers of the greatest message you have ever received—the message of hope and freedom. Hear it deep in your spirit. This is *our* sound. We carry the sound of freedom out to every precious person who has been struggling under a cloud of hopelessness to this day.

I wish I could describe to you the massive hit my inner man took when the word *cancer* was spoken over me. My dad had cancer and passed away at the young age of fifty. There have been other diagnoses of cancer in my family. Fear is real, and anxiety works itself out in ways that are far greater than you can explain to someone who has never experienced it. Dear friends bought me wall hangings that said "BRAVE" on them, and I so wanted this to be true, but it took me a little while. I am sure many of you have your own stories of personal tsunamis that hit you where you felt you could not draw a breath. When terror comes, it comes as a thief to your inner strength and your emotional resolve. And it hits you from your toes to your heart, in such a way that might prompt you to call an ambulance, because you feel you are going to die in that very moment.

I know that feeling. It does not feel *brave*, and it does not feel *courageous*. No, it feels like an intruder has come into the very place he is most unwelcome and has taken you hostage—along with all your hopes and dreams.

I cannot even imagine the fear that gripped the Jews back in Esther's time, as each day they woke up wondering if it would be their last. They were faced with the decision to base their belief in God and their faith in His promises or base their beliefs on what they saw with their eyes going on in the world around them.

We have all heard the saying, "I'll believe it when I see it." Well, that's not how belief works. That's not how faith works! Hebrews 11:1 tells us a different way to live: "Now faith is being sure of what we hope for and certain of what we do not see."

What do you believe today? Of what are you the most certain—even if you do not see it coming to pass in this very moment? It's easy to get sidetracked and discouraged in the world in which we live. In this world of constant information, of an ever-flowing stream of bad news—even if you are like me and sit on the side of the cup being half-full—it is easy to be dragged down to the level of how things appear.

Becoming certain of what you believe is *not* about striving; it is about resting and believing in His Word. It's about filling your home, your own sanctuary, your mind, and your thoughts with the words He has spoken over you—words of life and affirmation. To fill the air with worship is one of the easiest and most powerful ways to find the golden thread of God's goodness in the midst of dark days.

The Word of the Lord in 2 Chronicles 20:17 has this to say to you in the battles you are facing today: "You will not need to fight in this battle. Position yourselves, stand still and see the salvation of the LORD, who is with you. . . . Do not fear or be dismayed; tomorrow go out against them, for the LORD is with you" (NKJV).

Throughout the months when I was so sick, the people around me encouraged me—but it was and still is the Word of God that holds me secure in the midst of the storm.

What we talk about, declare, and confess always comes straight out of what we allow our minds to feed on. I have found on this journey that many people were actually at first very uncomfortable at my positive confession in the face of such a devastating diagnosis. When I began to speak what the Word of God said about my health and my body, they would frequently say, "Well, that's good, but what does the doctor say?"

In the book of Job, even those close to Job questioned the stance he took before God. But even though Job clearly stated that he could not *feel* God's presence, he still clung to the truth that he knew, based on what God had said and the character of the Lord, over and against the facts that he saw with his physical eyes. Job said:

I go east, but he is not there:
I go west, but I cannot find him.
I do not see him in the north, for he is hidden.
I look to the south, but he is concealed.
But he knows where I am going.
And when he tests me, I will come out as pure as gold.
For I have stayed on God's paths;
I have followed his ways and not turned aside.
I have not departed from his commands,
but have treasured his words more than daily food.

(JOB 23:8–12 NLT)

It is not simply the power of positive thinking that brings about courage and miracles in our lives; it is speaking the truth of the Word over and above the facts that we see. It is declaring life over death. The *real* fact is that death is swallowed up in victory! In a world that is grasping desperately for hope, we already have this hope—as the anchor for our souls:

Do not fret *or* have any anxiety about anything, but in every circumstance and in everything, by prayer and petition (definite requests), with thanksgiving, continue to make your wants known to God. And God's peace [shall be yours, that tranquil state of a soul assured of its salvation through Christ, and so fearing nothing from God and being content with its earthly lot of whatever sort that is, that peace] which transcends all understanding shall garrison and mount guard over your hearts and minds in Christ Jesus. (Philippians 4:6–7 AMPC)

Whatever is true, kind, and gracious—God's Word tells us to fix our minds on these things.

During my time of illness, I refused to even Google my diagnosis. I flat-out refused to fill my mind with the "what-ifs" of my disease. I refused to allow anyone else's story to negatively affect my sense of well-being. Instead I soaked in the words of life that were given to me from heaven.

I trust God that He has given me the best medical care for my particular situation. I listen to my doctors and do most of what they suggest. And I have continually reminded myself that it is God's Word that carries life: the miraculous is woven within every conversation, every declaration I make, and every belief I adhere to.

I know and believe that the finished work of Christ is *exactly that*: finished! I know that I know that I am the righteousness of God in Christ Jesus, and therefore, because Christ is alive in me, *all* sickness must flee. I encourage you, dear friends, to speak out what you know to be true! Let it become as bedrock in your spirit. Speak out the truth that God is at work in your life, and that you are even now seeing the miraculous come to pass—in Jesus' name! Speak out *faith* and *hope* in Christ, a hope and a faith that does not disappoint. Speak this out over your children: that they will thrive and flourish. Do not stay silent. Instead, turn your worship up, until it becomes louder than your fears!

THE MESSAGE OF HOPE

The thunderous message of hope that was carried on horseback in Esther's day was brought to all those who feared impending death, and this message renewed God's confirmed promise of life for His people. The message was one that valued the future and the legacy of the people, one that protected all the women and children among the Jews, and as you can imagine, it was a message of great gladness and joy.

Did you know that this message of hope is the very same message that God Himself has asked you and me to carry into His world? As Christ-followers, we carry the greatest message of hope that the world has ever seen. I pray that our motivation continues to be a love for people, a love based on how God Himself has loved us, and a commitment to living out the Great Commission as we are sent out into all the world—wherever God chooses to place us:

> Jesus, undeterred, went right ahead and gave his charge: "God authorized and commanded me to commission you: Go out and train everyone you meet, far and near, in this way of life, marking them by baptism in the threefold name: Father, Son, and Holy Spirit. Then instruct them in the practice of all I have commanded you. I'll be with you as you do this, day after day after day, right up to the end of the age." (Matthew 28:18–20 THE MESSAGE)

It is a humbling thought that our God uses each of us, as we continue in our assignments, to help each other and encourage each other. God's Word reminds us of this:

> Remember, our Message is not about ourselves; we're proclaiming Jesus Christ, the Master. All we are is messengers, errand runners from Jesus for you. It started when God said, "Light up the darkness!" and our lives filled up with light as we saw and understood God in the face of Christ, all bright and beautiful.
>
> If you only look at *us*, you might well miss the brightness. We carry this precious Message around in the unadorned clay pots of our ordinary lives. That's to prevent anyone from confusing God's incomparable power with us. As it is, there's not much chance of that. You know for yourselves that we're not much to look at. We've been surrounded and battered by troubles, but we're not demoralized; we're not sure what to do, but we know that God knows what to do; we've been spiritually terrorized, but God hasn't left our side; we've been thrown down, but we haven't broken. What they did to Jesus, they do to us—trial and

torture, mockery and murder; what Jesus did among them, he does in us—he lives! Our lives are at constant risk for Jesus' sake, which makes Jesus' life all the more evident in us. While we're going through the worst, you're getting in on the best!

We're not keeping this quiet, not on your life. Just like the psalmist who wrote, "I believed it, so I said it," we say what we believe. And what we believe is that the One who raised up the Master Jesus will just as certainly raise us up with you, alive. Every detail works to your advantage and to God's glory: more and more grace, more and more people, more and more praise! (2 Corinthians 4:5–13 THE MESSAGE)

A SUPERNATURAL EASE

On my fortieth birthday, I wanted to participate in a horse-riding adventure in the snowy mountains. So, Chloe, three close girl-friends, and I enrolled in a horse-riding camp. It was a five-star camping trip, believe me—and it was heavenly! I made so many great memories on that trip. But riding that horse at first was a bit uncomfortable for me—both physically and mentally! I certainly didn't begin the journey "at one" with my horse. He seemed so huge, literally too big for me—but the trainers said that he was my perfect size! After five days of working and practicing and fol-lowing through with everything my instructors told me to do, I finally began to see him like a playful puppy. Turns out, he *was* the perfect size for me. That horse and I eventually found our rhythm, and we even galloped and performed several little jumps, because we had become *so* comfortable with each other!

This is what it can feel like when you start walking in freedom *and* when you start helping others find freedom too. It can seem a little awkward at first, but the more you step out in courage, the easier it becomes. You can actually feel the supernatural ease that starts to flow when you hold on to Jesus and graciously walk into your purpose.

If you feel like you have no real part to play in God's glorious story of redemption, *stop*! Hear the sound of the gathering, galloping horses' hooves and know that the King has given His command: you are a part of the gathered forces, and it is time to announce that the time for freedom has arrived!

Don't waste another day waiting for all the circumstances in your life to line up before you find the courage to step out and do what you believe in your heart is important and true. I've learned to step out while still afraid. And as for courage? I have found that it eventually catches up with me.

> Be of good courage,
> And He shall strengthen your heart,
> All you who hope in the LORD.
>
> (PSALM 31:24 NKJV)

14

CHECKS AND BALANCES

What can you do to promote world peace?
Go home and love your children.
—Mother Teresa, Nobel Peace Prize speech, 1979

Recently I was talking to a young mother of two small children. She is also a pastor and worship leader, and because both of us are very passionate about our families, we had a *lot* to chat about! She was desperate for answers and insight into all that was going on in her heart, and after we got past the superficial details of our lives, the chatter became increasingly intense. She began to share with me her dissatisfaction and a growing sense of guilt in her spirit, as she felt she was compromising her role as a wife and a mother more and more by being so crazy-busy.

Dear friends, throughout this conversation, it felt as if my heart was going to burst out of my chest! I had battled the *exact same* feelings of guilt in varying degrees for so many years, and I felt like I had spent a thousand hours talking to God about this very issue.

Seasons and the calling of God on our lives has been an ongoing conversation for Mark and me, and we were so thankful when the Holy Spirit finally took us by the heart to what He had to say to us about this topic:

> Now, many of the Jews are opposed to the gospel, but their opposition has opened the door of the gospel to you who are not Jewish. Yet they are still greatly loved by God because their ancestors were divinely chosen to be his. And when God chooses someone and graciously imparts gifts to him, they are never rescinded. (Romans 11:28–29 TPT)

Some versions of this passage say that the gifts and callings that God gives us are given "without repentance." This means that God *knew what He was doing* when He gave you various passions and a skill and an ease in pursuing certain talents. And God knew what He was doing when He entrusted you with the treasured family in which He placed you. Our lives should morph and change with the rhythm of His plans—and His plans do include seasons. Sometimes we experience seasons when we have more freedom to work hard and to play hard, but then we also will go through seasons when it's time to hunker down and just flow with a gentler routine.

As I've said, I've always had a rather large capacity to work hard. I guess it comes from having to be self-sufficient from a very young age. This has been a great blessing in my life, of course, but it also has meant that I stayed immature for many, many years when it came to recognizing and responding to seasons of transition in my own life in a timely manner. This was also true for me when it came to parenting.

Even though I always had a deep desire for motherhood, I was shocked that it took longer than I would have thought for me to adjust well to that season of life. Ahhhh, transition. My babes may have grown and now have babes of their own, and this great blessing of family just gets richer—no less complicated I might add, but far greater than I ever imagined.

Have you noticed that each of us is *always* in a transition season in one or more areas of life at any given time? We are transitioning from youth to adult, from unmarried to married, from being a couple to being a family, from having one child to handling more, from not working to reentering the workforce, or vice versa. We move from parenting a baby to parenting a toddler to having a preschooler and then a little one at school. Before you know it, your kids are teen-agers, then they are leaving home and getting married. Then you are suddenly experiencing the birth of your grandchildren, monitoring the journey of your aging parents.

The constant change throughout life is endless. And so, too, the guilt can be endless. Maybe you feel that you are falling short of doing great through every transition *all the time*. I am sure there is not anyone reading this book who has not felt this way—even if you are not married, or if you are not a parent. Maybe you are single and just find it too hard to find the time to invest in the family and friends you already have.

No matter what stage of life you are in, this is what I know: if you are *consistently* too busy for your immediate "clan"—the precious ones who have been entrusted to your care—then you are too busy, period! I am not talking about busy seasons—we all have those seasons when we are in the trenches of life, with our sleeves rolled up and working hard—but when you continually sense that things in your life are far out of balance, you must begin to listen to the still, small voice of God that is asking you to address *balance* when it comes to your life and relationships.

Our family has, and I'm sure yours has, experienced tremendously crazy seasons over the years, and there are times when I have sensed such grace over our household during some incredibly busy and fruitful seasons. And yet there have been times, when without even realizing it, that I silenced the cry of my soul to just get on with it—and this always ended up hurting both me and my precious family.

I did eventually learn to listen to the hearts of my children, thankfully. I learned to follow the lead of my beloved husband, a man who needs space and time and long uninterrupted conversations with his wife. We learned not only our own needs and capacities through these times, but we also were able to learn the capacities of our little girls, what their love languages were, and their dreams and hopes. Our daughters have been our greatest teachers in life, over and over again.

"A false balance and dishonest business practices are extremely offensive to the LORD, but an accurate scale is His delight" (Proverbs 11:1 AMP). In other words, balance delights the heart of God. But the opposite of balance brings Him no pleasure at all.

So why do we continually find ourselves in this place of being overly busy and stressed and overworked and woefully out of balance? There are so many reasons. We need to work tirelessly to make ends meet or put kids through school. Or sometimes our hearts become so consumed at the idea of doing the right thing for *others* that we would never dare to say that we are at a breaking point or that we ourselves need help.

Many of us are without the choice to find a more even balance because of the chaos life has thrown at us. Even taking a much-needed one day off a week—has anyone ever heard of the Sabbath?—is very difficult for some people to do, as they are so used to running a hundred miles an hour. To even talk to anyone about maybe changing their pace sends them into influenza-like symptoms!

At other times, our lives are completely thrown out of balance because we truly believe that we should be able to keep up with everything we have going on. Doesn't everyone else manage such a breakneck pace?

I've had to ask myself some hard questions along the way:

Is this really God asking me to do this, or is this just me doing what I've always done?
Is God requiring this of me?

Through all my questions, all my failures, and all my successes, I have had to quiet my soul long enough to hear His gentle whisper speak to me and lead me in His way, which ultimately leads to peace.

"A just balance and [honest] scales are the LORD's; all the weights of the bag are His concern [established by His eternal principle]" (Proverbs 16:11 AMP). In this context, God's Word is telling us that the correct measures—the measure that God Himself gave us—will bring about the peace that accompanies His work. And so, in my own life, I can see that in order to achieve *His* correct balance, I must continue to look at those things to which I am giving my time, and I must make sure that it is not just me piling work up on myself. Considering the divine order for every single day of my life has become my goal. Working at the tasks *He* has given me to do is now the most important thing.

I don't know about you, but I need *fresh oil* every day! Yesterday's oil will not satisfy me for today's journey. Bishop T. D. Jakes says it this way: "Balance is part of your safety, and integrating it ensures wholeness."[1]

The part we play when it comes to serving God with the gifts He has given us is important, but the truth of a worshipful life is more so. You may find that in challenging the status quo in this area of your own life (without judging other people's decisions!), you may find a fair bit of resistance from those around you. But in the end, we are all accountable only for our own actions, and we will one day answer for them.

BEAUTY IN THE PURE AND SIMPLE

When we were making a huge family transition and moving into a new season of life, one of the blessings we experienced that made the transition so much easier was the birth of our first grand-daughter, Ava Pearl. Our eldest daughter, Amy, and her husband, Andrew ("Hoody"), brought this beautiful little girl into our lives. She was like a healing balm, helping us to negotiate the newness of our lives.

When a new season is on your horizon, it is *good* to stay focused on something that is pure and simple—for us, it was little Ava Pearl. We found that with Ava in our new life equation, some of the seemingly hard decisions we faced were actually made easier, as we focused on our lasting legacy rather than the immediacy of what we were feeling.

God is so kind to us all! He sees the beginning from the end, and as the most excellent keeper of our hearts, He also prepares us for the days yet to come. What we thought was a difficult time of transition became a training ground for what was about to happen next.

When Amy and Andrew were expecting our second grand-child, they were told that it looked like the new baby might have Down syndrome, as well as a hole in his heart. Fast-forward to the labor and delivery ward: I stood there on that day with Andrew and Amy, when she birthed this champion boy into the world. I watched as my daughter and her husband grabbed their beau-tiful newborn son, Roman Emmanuel Mark, and held him as they prayed. They spoke greatness over him for what seemed forever! I couldn't even see if this newest baby was a girl or a boy (we didn't learn Roman's gender before his birth); not even the nurses could get close to them—and no one rushed the parents through their time of prayer over their new baby. It was a sacred moment that I will never forget!

Roman Emmanuel did not have Down syndrome, and neither did he have a hole in his heart. When he left the hospital with his parents, he was proclaimed a perfectly healthy baby boy. Yet at about eighteen months old, we started noticing that he was becoming less and less responsive to normal noises, voices, or loud music—which had been his favorite thing to listen and dance to. Hoody and Amy knew something wasn't right, but after seeing a few doctors who were the best in their field, all Amy and Andrew knew was that Roman's hearing was perfect, so that was not the issue. What we eventually came to learn soon after that time was that Roman was on the "autism spectrum"—and life as we knew it was about to change dramatically.

I will not go into all the details, as this is Amy and Andrew's story to tell in full someday, and I am sure they will. But this was an unexpected season in life. At times it has been very confusing. There have been many opinions regarding why Roman's behavior started to change so dramatically, but we know that this precious little boy is a complete miracle and gift from God. And God knew what He was doing when He planned Roman's days before He ever crafted this little boy in his mother's womb. God also knows the best way for Roman to move forward in life into all He has planned for Roman's future. But in the meantime, as a family, we have all done our very best to love and support Amy, Hoody, Ava, Roman, and Ruthie (their youngest) in this season, and we are determined to move at a pace that is doable for this precious family.

This season, which had been so unexpected, has now become so magnificent, as Roman continues to teach us how to look at the world differently. We have learned that life doesn't come to us in straight lines. We now know that just because a different season is upon us, that does not mean that it has to be a negative thing. Roman loves with absolute abandon, with the whole of his being. He doesn't sweat the small stuff, and he laughs with his entire body. I know that he is chatting with the angels continually. He swims like a fish, he has the energy of a thousand kangaroos, and he can sing like the coolest rapper ever. I could go on and on. And Amy and Andrew? Well, they simply shine in their role as Roman's parents and cheerleaders.

Roman's story seemed at times like a fast-approaching cloud that tried to block the greatest rainbow we had ever seen—but we know that the greatest days in his story are unfolding day by day, miracle by miracle.

THE NEXT STORM

So, for our family, while negotiating this new life with Roman, while finding our new rhythm, our new normal, another new season—the next storm—was forming on the horizon, and it was a doozy. Breast cancer. It hit without warning.

In the midst of it all, God's Word holds steady and true:

> So shall they fear
> The name of the LORD from the west,
> And His glory from the rising of the sun;
> When the enemy comes in like a flood,
> The Spirit of the LORD will lift up a standard against him.
>
> (ISAIAH 59:19 NKJV)

Yes, the enemy and his evil plans for us swept into our lives like a flood—like a fierce flood that crashed over us while we were walking out these new days with Roman. By then the Hood family had grown, with the addition of Ruthie Feather, and Chloe was dating a handsome young man named Hosanna. Zoe was thriving in her new environment, and church was bursting at the seams. Life was full and wonderful. This unwelcome diagnosis was serious, and it swept us off our feet, leaving us in a daze of anguish, dealing with a new level of fear trying to completely take us out.

But then, surrounded by men and women of prayer and faith, we received communion together, we were anointed with oil, and we were prayed over—continually and forcefully. With authority. With love. With compassion. With the beautiful golden thread of the Holy Spirit's kindness leading and guiding the people around us who held us up, day in and day out.

And so we hunkered down with our burgeoning hope. We held on to Christ, our anchor, with every breath that we took. My children wept with fear, and yet at the same time we were all carried in God's astounding love through that entire season. My husband was our captain. He sailed the ship of our family through this greatest of storms with unyielding hope in our future, keeping his own fears between him and the Lord and a few trusted friends.

For me, as a wife and a mother and grandmother, I realized that some of the seasons we had walked through before this time— seasons both hard and easy—were a training ground through several years leading up to this crisis. I have had to watch my daughters dig their own wells in God in this season, and even though I would have loved to have spared them all the pain of this time, the truth is that deep wells don't come easy. God knows what He is doing in each of our lives as He carries us through and strengthens us in the battle.

As a family, we have emerged as a strong unit, still together, better than ever. We do have a few scars, but we have a deep sense of gratitude that the grace of God is as astounding as it seems to be—and yes, it seems too good to be true most of the time! It's funny to me now, that most of the things I would battle in my mind and heart, about loyalty and about what God was speaking to my heart, the wind of adversity suddenly blew completely away. Much of the dross that I had left over from my emotional garden—gone! So many things that I could not previously get my head around, all of a sudden were simply of no stress to me, and my new path forward was made so very clear.

When Jonathan David and Melissa Helser from Bethel wrote the song "No Longer Slaves," it was like the golden thread of heaven in my heart. It gave me strength through the pain after my treatments, and it kept giving Mark a rush of kingdom adrenaline as he asked our church to sing this every week for I don't know how long. How grateful I am for people who labor over songs and art and messages and photography. All those things helped me to continue to bring balance to my inner man, giving me the strength to hold my head high in God's presence.

My dear friends, through all the seasons of our family, in good times and in hard times, God has held each of us in the palm of His hands. When I think about the fact that our Lord *literally* is the Alpha and the Omega, the beginning and the end of all things, my heart, which continually longs for more of Him, simply settles down in a greater trust that He knows what He is doing in my life and in the lives of our cherished family. During each of the times when I have made myself too busy, and yet I was thinking I was doing the right thing, I have to sow those things into God's eternal ocean of mercy and grace. And the "parent guilt" or the "friend guilt" that we all wrestle with? Well, today is a new day for that too!

Let's each of us choose to plant some new seeds of love and time today—into the people around us—so that in the seasons ahead, our harvest will be plentiful. God has the most amazing way of redeeming our days—better than we could have ever expected! We cannot change the things we may regret, but we sure can change the way we approach life into tomorrow, the next day, and the day after that.

So I will restore to you the years that the swarming locust has
    eaten,
The crawling locust,
The consuming locust,
And the chewing locust,
My great army which I sent among you.
You shall eat in plenty and be satisfied,
And praise the name of the LORD your God,
Who has dealt wondrously with you;
And My people shall never be put to shame.
Then you shall know that I am in the midst of Israel:
I am the LORD your God
And there is no other.
My people shall never be put to shame.

(JOEL 2:25–27 NKJV)

I pray over our unseen lives of worship, our personal commitment to our families, and our dedication to praying for one another.
I pray for our kids, for our lives that are in times of transition, for
those times when trouble comes to us, that we don't just keep on
living so loudly that we drown out the Spirit's call to put those
things that are not right in order. And I pray that as we draw closer
to Jesus, we would *listen* as the Holy Spirit speaks to our hearts
about bringing change where change is needed, about doing things
God's way without simply following the patterns of this world.

15

FOREVER
THANKFUL

*This way of seeing our Father in everything
makes life one long thanksgiving, and gives
a rest of heart, and, more than that, a
happiness of spirit, that is unspeakable.*
—Hannah Whitall Smith, *The
Christian's Secret of a Happy Life*

It seems to me that the older I get, the more I realize the importance of living a life that is founded in thanksgiving. Interestingly, in the culture of the Old Testament, the word most often used in place of *thanks* was *praise*. It literally means to tell one another what God has done. An even more accurate description would be, "I will tell of Your name."

"Since we are receiving our rights to an unshakable kingdom, we should be extremely thankful and offer God the purest worship that delights His heart as we lay down our lives in absolute surrender, filled with awe" (Hebrews 12:28 TPT). In response to knowing who we are in Christ, knowing our rights as partakers of an unshakable kingdom, then our lives lived in surrender to the will of God must be lived out in thanksgiving.

Wow. It is easy to be thankful when all is well, but learning to give God thanksgiving and praise no matter what is going on in your world? That is part of the sacrifice of praise and part of the miracle we get to experience every time we bring thanks regardless of how we may *feel*. This is what life in the Spirit looks like. Life is to be lived with an awareness again of this golden thread of God's heart toward us and the reality of His powerful presence, even when it feels like the earth is caving in.

People can say careless things while you are walking through fire. Usually it's not because they are mean or wanting to harm you, but it's often because they don't know what to say, and so thoughtlessly they revert to vocal malfunctions: "Um, ahh, oh well, God is good, eh?" I have found myself in this situation, and it never ends well.

Don't get me wrong: God *is* good—this is never in question—but please allow the hearts of hurting people to receive His truth via the wind of the Spirit, not via the hammer of self-righteousness.

I had to learn to bring thanksgiving into the midst of my physical suffering, of physically feeling like I could die almost immediately, in the midst of seeing those I loved suffer, in the midst of a huge lack of understanding. Someone told me to thank God for the cancer. Let me be honest here. I never once thanked God for the cancer. He did not give me cancer; it wasn't a gift of love from Him to teach me a lesson.

No, I felt no grace to thank God for cancer. But I have thanked Him a million times for the other gifts I received along the way: the gift of His presence, the gift of the golden threads of His nature that knit me close to His heart. I have thanked Him for the gift of healing, which I receive as I declare Psalm 91 over my body daily. I have thanked Him for the grace to walk through the fire, for the gift of eternal life whenever it is my time to enter into His presence. I have thanked Him for the most precious gift of family and friends, which I now treasure and appreciate in ways that I might never have before my cancer diagnosis. I thank Him for the many brave people I have had the honor to meet during this season. I thank Him for the gift of time, which I now treat with great respect. I thank Him for the gift of my church family, the bride of Christ, whom I have always loved and feel immensely protective of. Can you see the difference here?

God is not asking us to be fake and full of whimsical pretense. He is asking us to posture our hearts toward His kindness, of which there is no end.

Thanksgiving is a choice, a decision we make based on the Word of God and faith in God. It's a stance of the heart, the entry point to His gates. Remember, thanksgiving is *giving thanks*. Thanksgiving is not just about *feeling* thankful, but it is about expressing that thankfulness, even if in the beginning this response is small and maybe done with hesitation.

> In everything give thanks, for this is the will of God in Christ Jesus for you. (1 Thessalonians 5:18 NKJV)

In *everything*. Whether on your knees in silence while your heart breathes a desperate thank you, whether with outstretched hands and triumphant singing, whether in giving of your firstfruits financially, whether in service to God's house—the list goes on and on. In whatever season, in whatever moment, part of learning to grow in God is to be thankful. Thanksgiving literally makes a way, a path into the courts of God.

> Enter his gates with thanksgiving;
> go into his courts with praise.
> Give thanks to him and praise his name.

> For the LORD is good.
> His unfailing love continues forever,
> and his faithfulness continues to each generation.
>
> (PSALM 100:4–5 NLT)

> Through Him then, let us continually offer up a sacrifice of praise to God, that is, the fruit of lips that give thanks to His name. (Hebrews 13:15 NASB)

I love that here the writer is saying that this is done by Him, by the power of the Spirit. Give thanks.

So, when it comes to giving thanks, let me tell you what has made the greatest difference in our lives. During the last ten years, Mark and I have rediscovered the power of receiving communion, the power of remembering the broken body and precious blood of Jesus through which He paid the ultimate price for us. We have committed in our hearts to never go through the motions while partaking of this powerful and sacred moment of remembrance. When Jesus modeled the moment of gathering at the table around communion, before He received the elements, He gave thanks.

> For I pass on to you what I received from the Lord himself. On the night when he was betrayed, the Lord Jesus took some bread and gave thanks to God for it. Then he broke it in pieces and said, "This is my body, which is given for you. Do this in remembrance of me." (1 Corinthians 11:23–24 NLT)

I cannot imagine what was going on in the heart of Jesus as He led His friends around this space, knowing He was leading them around the purpose of His death, which was all still immediately in front of Him. But even as fully God and fully man, He still gave thanks. His heart remained firmly fixed on His purpose and on God's plan. Thanksgiving is far more powerful than we realize. A thankful heart finds life easier to contend with, as your thank you keeps you tied to the golden thread of God's faithfulness.

> And whatever you do, in word or deed, do everything in the name of the Lord Jesus, giving thanks to God the Father through him. (Colossians 3:17 ESV)

As we partake of communion and bring our thanksgiving to the Lord, let's remember that through the victory of the cross, the greatest expression of God's love, we live and move in the power of resurrection life.

G. K. Chesterton said: "I would maintain that thanksgiving is the highest form of thought, and that gratitude is happiness doubled by wonder."

One of my daily personal disciplines is, before I put my feet on the floor each morning, I thank God for the gift of another day. I ask that He would use me in whatever way He wants to use me. Thanksgiving sets my heart, it sets my stance, and it reserves gratefulness as the undertone to how I choose to walk out my life.

When I think about everything I have been given—the golden thread of the grace and mercy of God, which is completely undeserved by *any* of us!—how could I be anything *but* thankful? I used to try to apologize for what God has done in my life (somehow I thought that this was being humble), but I guess after walking through the last few years, what I see as truly valuable has been stripped back, and what I now focus on daily is very clear to me. I know my lane, and I refuse to apologize for God's mercy and grace. I now *know* that if my heart continually remains thankful and passionate for His kingdom to come in my life, then my life will be lived to bring Him glory.

> Be cheerful no matter what; pray all the time; thank God no matter what happens. This is the way God wants you who belong to Christ Jesus to live. (1 Thessalonians 5:16–18 THE MESSAGE)

God is so worthy of our gratitude and thankfulness! Our parents teach us from a very young age to say "please" and "thank you" as a common courtesy. How common should it be for us to thank our Creator, the great God of the universe, for all the gifts we receive from Him each day? When we praise Him, we honor Him for who He is in our lives: He is not only our Creator, He is our Provider, Sustainer, Savior, Restorer, the One who holds us in the palm of His hand.

In addition, God promises to be with us through every season, every storm, of our lives. He lifts us up on the wind of His Spirit, above the storms and cares of this world, and He shields us as we walk through problems and attacks of the enemy, by the power of the Spirit of God. In fact, if you are finding it hard even to lift your head toward heaven in this time and season, let me encourage you to allow the worship of God to carry your soul heavenward. Sometimes the decision to worship is the only way forward. With all my heart, I encourage you to make the decision to bring thankfulness into the equation of your life's current circumstances, and by faith, enter the courts of God with praise.

A grateful spirit is a satisfied spirit. I think that in order to be fully alive, you've got to learn how to be fully satisfied. Yield yourself to God's gracious care. Unite your heart with His and make His will your own. You won't regret it.

Settle in to Him.
Enter into His rest.
Breathe in His Spirit and experience His peace.
And then thank Him for who He is and all He has done
    for you.

I encourage you today to determine in your heart to have an attitude of gratefulness and thanksgiving at all times, for who knows what lies on the other side of your obedience?

16

SOAR

*One can never consent to creep when
one feels an impulse to soar.*
—HELEN KELLER, *THE STORY OF MY LIFE*

LIVING IN A COASTAL AREA HAS BROUGHT A NEW AWARENESS TO
me of seasons and weather patterns, of the breathtaking sunrises
and sunsets that are majestically painted before my eyes every
day, of the fierceness of the storms that sweep in from the ocean,
and of the peace that comes after these storms. I am inspired as I
watch eagles fly—fearlessly and weightlessly—during the fiercest
of storms. They simply spread their wings and do what they were
born to do, no matter what is swirling all around them, while I,
a mere human, run for shelter. I watch them soar and dip with
seemingly no effort at all, and I notice that the very winds that are
buffeting me actually cause them to rise to even greater heights.

Listen to the words of the prophet in Isaiah 40:

> Why would you ever complain, O Jacob,
> or, whine, Israel, saying,
> "GOD has lost track of me.
> He doesn't care what happens to me"?
> Don't you know anything? Haven't you been listening?
> God doesn't come and go. God lasts.
> He's Creator of all you can see or imagine.
> He doesn't get tired out, doesn't pause to catch his breath.
> And he knows everything, inside and out.
> He energizes those who get tired,
> gives fresh strength to dropouts.
> For even young people tire and drop out,
> young folk in their prime stumble and fall.
> But those who wait upon God get fresh strength.
> They spread their wings and soar like eagles,
> They run and don't get tired,
> they walk and don't lag behind.
>
> (VV. 27–31 THE MESSAGE)

We all have within our spirits the impulse to soar. Consider these timeless words:

> He has made everything beautiful and appropriate in its time. He has also planted eternity [a sense of divine purpose] in the human heart [a mysterious longing which nothing under the sun can satisfy, except God]—yet man cannot find out (comprehend, grasp) what God has done (His overall plan) from the beginning to the end. (Ecclesiastes 3:11 AMP)

Often the frustration you feel on the inside is there because you *know* that there is *so* much more purpose for you in this life than what you are currently experiencing! When your current season feels stuck, that transition can seem like it takes forever to get through. And it can bring a pain and a frustration that can be all-consuming.

Maybe you are in this season due to circumstances beyond your control. If that is the case, sometimes it can seem like a dark cloud of discouragement has descended over your spirit that won't seem to lift. At other times, we feel this way because we have unmet expectations that can ultimately build into resentment.

Maybe you have dreams for your life that keep recurring and you've done nothing about them yet. Unfulfilled dreams can certainly make you feel stuck—especially when you feel powerless to fulfill them.

Paul provided some insight into how the Holy Spirit can help us when we go through these times of discouragement:

> You, however, are not in the realm of the flesh but are in the realm of the Spirit, if indeed the Spirit of God lives in you. And if anyone does not have the Spirit of Christ, they do not belong to Christ. But if Christ is in you, then even though your body is subject to death because of sin, the Spirit gives life because of righteousness. And if the Spirit of him who raised Jesus from the dead is living in you, he who raised Christ from the dead will also give life to your mortal bodies because of his Spirit who lives in you. (Romans 8:9–11 NIV)

Because we are made in the image of God, it is good to remember that we were made to rise. We were made to live free in Christ, despite the weights of this world.

This way of life *is* possible, my dear friend. It is possible *in Him*. The Spirit of God who raised Jesus from the dead *is alive in us*! That's a whole lot of resurrection power we have available to us to make amazing changes in our lives.

When Isaiah 40 gives us the glorious picture of the eagle soaring above the circumstances of life, it is not showing us a picture of an eagle restrained in the confines of a zoo. This amazing creature is not meant to be held captive; it is not meant to fly with its wings tucked underneath it, only going around and around within the circle of imprisonment.

No! The eagle, just like you and me, was created to be a majestic, intricate creature—and yet any one of us, just like an eagle living in confined spaces, can find ourselves stuck under the confines of some sort of captivity. We are held captive by our thinking or our experience, by fatigue, by stress, or any other enemies of our calling that would hinder our destiny in the Spirit. When our majestic design becomes hindered or even simply shrunk down by our unique struggles, we can lose sight of the calling, the destiny that the Lord has for us.

This is not God's will for our lives! We were born to *soar*!

The glorious eagle, when it is being what it was born to be, glides as high as the mountains; it flies hundreds of miles with absolute ease. The eagle is the original storm rider, drifting effortlessly, fearlessly, through the fiercest of storms—when it is free to fulfill its destiny. But when it has lived in captivity for a long while, even if it is later released, it won't take flight. If an eagle has experienced sustained confinement, it loses its ability to live as it was designed to live.

SEASONS OF WAITING

Those who wait for the LORD [who expect, look for, and hope
    in Him]
Will gain new strength and renew their power;
They will lift up their wings [and rise up close to God] like
    eagles [rising toward the sun];

They will run and not become weary,
They will walk and not grow tired.

(Isaiah 40:31 amp)

In any season of rebuilding, the key for us to be made whole again is found in *waiting*. Waiting on God and in God is actually a gift. Maybe you don't like the way the gift has been presented, but it is in the waiting that you will begin to see facets of God's love and heart toward you that you may have never seen before.

Waiting on the Lord means to "attend to, to wait upon." The word *wait* here is the Hebrew word *quvah*, which means "to wait, to expect, to wait eagerly, to look." It is not passive waiting, but waiting while watching, receiving, growing, and expecting. It involves action!

Even during the last few years, as I have had to wait for my physical strength to be renewed—which has *greatly* tested my patience—I have had no choice but to dig deep into God and His loving arms during the waiting period. I have had to keep what I have seen and learned from Him in the forefront of my mind throughout this seemingly dim season, and the whole process has actually caused a new light and life to be birthed within my spirit. But it has not been easy. It requires me to make a choice. Most times I have chosen well, but there have been days when I have either nursed self-pity or allowed physical weakness or pain to tell me how to feel in my heart and my spirit. But in the end, neither of these choices allowed my spirit to flourish or my body to rest well. Choose life in the times of waiting in your life!

Wait passionately for God,
don't leave the path.
He'll give you your place in the sun
while you watch the wicked lose it.

(Psalm 37:34 the message)

This verse does not imply inactivity; rather, it instructs us to be passionate during our times of waiting! All our hope and salvation are found in Him, and we must continue to actively seek His face, even while we are waiting for Him to bring our destinies to pass.

When we wait on the Lord, the Word tells us that our strength will be "renewed." The Hebrew word for *renewed* actually means "to revive, to cause to flourish again, to restore that which has been destroyed."

And not only are we renewed, but we are to mount up on wings like eagles. One commentary actually says that "they shall put forth fresh feathers like the moulting eagle." Various studies on eagles' behavior shows that these majestic creatures will live and retain their strength to a very old age, and then, unlike many other birds, the eagle will hide away while it molts in its later years. During that time of molting, the eagle renews its feathers—and with that its youth is restored! And the majestic bird comes out again refreshed, with new feathers, ready for a new season of life.

How like our amazing God to use this incredible bird to demonstrate for us what He wants to do in each of our lives! New feathers for a new season of life? Yes, please!

Psalm 103 reveals this picture yet again:

> With my whole heart, with my whole life,
> and with my innermost being,
> I bow in wonder and love before you, the holy God!
> Yahweh, you are my soul's celebration.
> How could I ever forget the miracles of kindness
> you've done for me?
> You kissed my heart with forgiveness, in spite of all I've done.
> You've healed me inside and out from every disease.
> You've rescued me from hell and saved my life.
> You've crowned me with love and mercy.
> You satisfy my every desire with good things.

You've supercharged my life so that I soar again
like a flying eagle in the sky!

(vv. 1–5 TPT)

We can use the differing seasons, and even the storms of life, to rise to greater dimensions in the Spirit. The eagle rides the wind and circles higher and higher toward the sky—without effort. She just spreads her wings and lets the wind carry her through the sky.

God promises to be with us through every season, every storm, of our lives. He lifts us up on the wind of His Spirit, above the storms and cares of this world, and He lifts us up above all the problems and attacks of the enemy, by the power of the Spirit of God.

I discovered one further interesting piece of information about eagles. These birds do not eat dead things. They feed only on fresh prey. Vultures eat dead animals—but eagles will not.

What a radical lesson for us to grasp about God's will for us in every season and circumstance of life! In your waiting period, be careful with what you feed your eyes and your ears. As human beings, we tend to grab on to all kinds of random things when we are looking desperately for a fast way out of our current season of pain and trouble. But these things, if they are not from the life-giving Spirit of the living God, can bring more harm to our lives than good.

So, how do we wait on the Lord?

Taking the time to wait *on* God and wait *with* God is probably one of the greatest disciplines you'll ever learn as a Christ follower. As we draw near to Him, intentionally and eagerly, the Word says that He then draws near to us. He continually confirms our identity in Him. He continues to reveal how much we are loved by Him. A regular, daily, beautiful, heavenly encounter is literally one prayer away. Find a place in your day, every day, in your home and in your heart, to meet with the Lord. Find your personal prayer "war room": grab your Bible and a notebook, and then be still before the Lord.

As you step into a new season of soaring while waiting, learn to step into Him and His love for you first. God doesn't need our strength. We need His! The art of waiting well is found in surrender. When we surrender, we find a new clarity. Out of surrender we learn to receive the golden thread of His mercy and grace, as the time of prayerful waiting refines us and keeps us on our knees.

Everything in the kingdom of God is sustainable, so if you are feeling worn out and weary, then take a good look at what it is you are applying yourself to. Maybe you've picked the wrong things purely because of frustration with your current situation.

If that is the case, then let go of those things! Focus on what the Lord has for you instead. That is where you will find His strength to endure the time of waiting:

> Trust GOD from the bottom of your heart;
>> don't try to figure out everything on your own.
> Listen for GOD's voice in everything you do, everywhere
>> you go;
>> he's the one who will keep you on track.
> Don't assume that you know it all.
>> Run to GOD! Run from evil!
> Your body will glow with health,
>> your very bones will vibrate with life!
>
> (PROVERBS 3:5–8 THE MESSAGE)

We are to trust in the Lord, no matter what is going on.

> In God I trust; I shall not be afraid.
>> What can man do to me?
>
> (PSALM 56:11 ESV)

What if worry is the thing that is clipping your "eagle's wings" right now? Let go of it, as Jesus asks you to do:

"Don't let your hearts be troubled. Trust in God, and trust also in me." (John 14:1 NLT)

Jesus was not saying that we should live in denial of the problems or difficulties that we face through life's different seasons. And He was not saying that He doesn't care about the things that are troubling us. Jesus was saying: "Don't worry or be anxious! Instead, trust Me to help you with the difficult situations that you encounter in this life."

One of my favorite writers, Max Lucado, said this: "Our prayers may be awkward. Our attempts may be feeble. But since the power of prayer is in the one who hears it and not in the one who says it, our prayers do make a difference."[1]

Maybe this is a season in your life when, like the eagle, your new feathers are being applied to take you into a new season—while you wait, pray, are thankful, and believe. Be patient and trust: your new strength is on its way.

17

LIFT UP YOUR
HANDS

Jesus! It is the name which moves the harps
of heaven to melody . . . a gathering up of
the hallelujahs of eternity in five letters.
—CHARLES SPURGEON, *MORNING AND EVENING*

DEAR ONES, DID YOU KNOW THAT THERE IS NOTHING MORE PRECIOUS, nothing more secure, nothing more inspiring than knowing that the Maker of heaven and earth desires to be with you? Whatever you are facing today, you need to remember to remember this fact. Take the time necessary to make room for His Word, to keep the reminders of His presence ever before you, to allow the Lord Jesus to speak to you and encourage you in every situation. He is longing to be with you, to lead you to where He is and to speak tenderly to you.

LIFT UP!

Lift up your head. Lift up your eyes. Lift up your hands and receive what He has for you.

As He begins to light you up from the inside, you can then walk into *any* situation without fear, because the river of God is inside you, always ready to bring life and healing through the limitless golden thread that flows through our lives—the love and mercy of God.

We must learn to listen for His voice, talk with Him about our worries and cares, involve Him in our day—every day—and then put ourselves into the position of being available to be filled with His extravagant love for us.

In John 15:9, we are told that Jesus loves *each of us* in the exact same way and to the exact same depth as the Father God has loved Him—*His very own Son*! And then our Lord instructs us to "remain in that love."

Hebrews 4:16 adds the term *boldly* to our instruction to enter into the presence of God and dwell there: Come boldly into His presence. Practicing the presence of God simply involves loving God, pursuing Him and His heart for us, receiving that love, and then involving Him in every part of our lives each day. We can halt our practice of the presence of God by thinking that our life is all about what *we* are doing for God and how *we* are serving Him.

Lord, help us to continually keep our focus completely on *You* and what *You* want to do in us and through us.

GUARDING TIME WITH THE BELOVED

You need to be deliberate. I have times set apart in my week in order to come away from the busyness and hectic schedules of life, in order to meet with the Lord. And when people ask me to do certain things that would conflict with this time, I usually say, "sorry, I have another appointment then." Because you can guarantee, if you have set apart time to just *be* with Jesus, that a hundred other things will come up to try to take its place in your life and schedule.

For this reason, I have to diligently guard the time I plan to spend with my Beloved. Within life's walk, from day to day, I seek to involve Him in every detail of my life; I talk to God and include Him in pretty much everything. I know that He is already there inside of me, and so I make sure I include Him in everything going on in my world.

Whether in the physical or in the spiritual, it is my intent to lift my head, lift my eyes, and lift my hands throughout my day.

Start your day praising and exalting Him for who He is, and for His faithfulness, naming off as many good things as come to your mind. This time of praise and worship will not be the same for everyone nor will it happen at the exact same time of day. When you are in different seasons of life, it may change in your own life, as well. This should never be about a formula; it's completely about living *in* Him—enjoying Him and enjoying Him living in you.

Perhaps most challenging in our noisy world, I do my best to listen. During this time that I intentionally spend with Him, God may remind me to call someone and encourage that person, or He may give me a specific scripture to encourage me in whatever I am facing that day. And every week there seems to be another big moment, when three or four people will text Mark and me a Scripture verse, and we are always astonished when God has been speaking to us about that exact verse throughout the days before the texts began.

Every day as we "remember to remember" God's active working in our lives, there are more and more opportunities to be led by the Holy Spirit to speak to someone—and most often these people will share a story about how they had just been crying out to God for help. When we maintain a constant awareness that we are *in Him and that He is in us*, all our circumstances, our whole day, is lived *in* Him—because we are! Always thank Him for being present in the little things of life, in the ordinary moments when His presence spills over and blesses you unexpectedly.

The secret to living in this presence of God's golden thread of love and mercy, to jump into the flow of His Spirit, and to share all this with other people is to *know* that His presence is with you and *in* you always. We are one with the Father as we abide in the Vine; no one and nothing can ever separate us from Him or His love for us.

Because He lives within us, let's include Him, welcome Him, and acknowledge Him in every part of our lives—big and small—because He is there and because He wants to share life with us.

I KNOW THAT I KNOW

I pray that over the course of this book, you have a clearer picture in your own life about the goodness of God and this golden thread of His nature that finds itself woven deeply into our framework, continuing to call us deeper into Himself. You have read that throughout the struggles and challenges and changing seasons of my life, I have had to wrestle with my flesh and my heart, but these are the times I am now so very grateful for, as I had to learn to trust Him on a whole new level.

King David prophesied the following words about Jesus:

> I continually see the Lord in front of me.
> He's at my right hand, and I am never shaken.
> No wonder my heart is glad and my glory celebrates!
> My mouth is filled with his praises,

and I have hope that my body will live
because you will not leave my soul among the dead,
nor will you allow your sacred one to experience decay.
For you have revealed to me the pathways to life,
and seeing your face fills me with euphoria!

(ACTS 2:25–28 TPT)

Living face-to-face with a God who simply cannot turn His face away from you, living daily with the stunning and unrelenting power of the Holy Spirit in your life, living your life in the very presence of the Lord who walks with you every step of the way and who fills your mortal body with *dynamos* power: this can be difficult to explain to someone who has never experienced it. Oh, but I know that I know and have experienced the power of the Spirit available to strengthen us—the very same resurrection power that raised Christ from the dead. He is here and ready to empower us to walk through anything and everything we might face in this world.

As I have leaned in to His presence through worship, I have found, over and over again, that worship itself does not fully and completely satisfy the desire I have for more of Jesus, but it does give me greater clarity, as my heart yearns for more of Him. Worship digs the well of my heart ever deeper and deeper, so much so that the things of this world that I may have started to long for begin to take their rightful place in direct subordination to the love and the purposes of God in my life.

Psalm 124 stands as a stunning testament to many of our own life stories, as it speaks to the truth of a God who longs to be with us, who never leaves us or forsakes us:

What if God had not been on our side? Let all Israel admit this!
What if God had not been there for us?
Our enemies, in their violent anger,

would have swallowed us up alive!
The nations, with their flood of rage, would have swept us
    away
and we would have drowned,
perished beneath their torrent of terror!
We can praise God over and over that he never left us!
God wouldn't allow the terror of our enemies to defeat us.
We are free from the hunter's trap;
their snare is broken and we have escaped!
For the same God who made everything,
our Creator and our mighty maker,
he himself is our helper and defender!

(VV. 1–8 TPT)

I see this in the writings of King David in the Psalms, and I also experience it in the Gospels, which paint a portrait of King Jesus, the Lord who knew His mission and who stayed attentive to it. But they also picture the Savior who is interruptible, who is always looking into our lives and into the margins of our world for those who have been cast aside or who have been forced into the deep and lonely edges of society. He is our Helper and Defender! He weaves the golden thread of His love and mercy throughout each of our lives, entwining us together in the golden garment of His grace.

Pain attracts the grace of God. Sin, also, attracts His grace and mercy.

You may find yourself in a prolonged season of pain at this time. I do know, and I truly understand, how hard it is to focus on much else when your entire body and soul is racked with unrelenting pain—whether physical, emotional, or spiritual anguish. But let the following words seep deep into your wounds and bring a healing salve to your spirit:

And now my head shall be lifted up above my enemies all
　　around me;
Therefore I will offer sacrifices of joy in His tabernacle;
I will sing, yes, I will sing praises to the LORD.

(PSALM 27:6 NKJV)

Lift up your head. Allow the Holy Spirit to pour into you this day His strength and His healing power. In your current circumstances, this may seem like a sacrifice, but on the other side of your obedience to this hope that He asks you to maintain are the rewards of God's promises, His unexpected Holy showing up to thread the golden strand of mercy and love in every season of your life. The glory of God is drawing close.

And may I encourage you, if you have never opened your heart to the love of God, to do it today.

And what is God's "living message"? It is the revelation of faith for salvation, which is the message that we preach. For if you publicly declare with your mouth that Jesus is Lord and believe in your heart that God raised him from the dead, you will experience salvation. The heart that believes in him receives the gift of the righteousness of God—and then the mouth gives thanks to salvation. For the Scriptures encourage us with these words: "Everyone who believes in him will never be disappointed." (Romans 10:9–11 TPT)

He is as close as a breath away. And as you walk out your life in faith, look for a good Bible-believing church. There you will find your family of faith and those who will journey with you on life's great adventure.

God can do anything, you know—far more than you could ever imagine or guess or request in your wildest dreams! He does it not by pushing us around but by working within us, His Spirit deeply and gently within us.

> Glory to God in the church!
> Glory to God in the Messiah, in Jesus!
> Glory down all the generations!
> Glory through all millennia! Oh, yes!
>
> (EPHESIANS 3:20–21 THE MESSAGE)

THANK YOU!

I NEVER DREAMED I WOULD BE AN AUTHOR. ACTUALLY, I NEVER dreamed I would be a songwriter either. But these are the tools I have been given to help communicate the story of my life, and the way God intercepted my jumbled heart and encountered me in a way that has left me radically changed and with a deep longing for more. But the journey is always about others, and the way our lives entwine for the glory of God, and so I will do my best to thank some of people who have walked with me and without whom none of this would be possible.

First, thank you to my ever-loving and awesome hubby, Mark, who definitely had me at hello, and who has been cheering me on for so many years as a wife and mum and in all other aspects of life. He has never made me feel like I need to hide or small myself down because I am a female, and as a father of three daughters (Amy, Chloe, and Zoe), he has cheered us all on in our hearts' desires and dreams, and for this I am eternally grateful. I love that our journey thus far has been so diverse, I love that we are all in it together, and I love that you keep leading me into adventure. I love that we build together, whether it's our family or our church or our businesses or our home. And whether it's on public platforms or around our table, you are the same kind and fun human. I love you deeply and forever.

To our kids and grandkids—Amy, Andrew, Chloe, Hosanna,

Zoe, Ava, Roman, Ruthie Feather and Thea Mae—your lives are my inspiration. Now, I know we have promised five dollars for every mention of your names from a public platform, and I know we must owe you a lot of money by now. But I cannot help myself. And I am sure that this book will mean I owe you a whole lot more! I love that our family table is the highlight of our daily and weekly traditions that I know we all hold as sacred. I love how now, in this season, you are our children but also our best friends. You are all so gifted and selfless, and I know and understand that as pastors' kids, you live in a lane that has to be paved with grace that only those walking on it will understand. But you do so with passion and wit, and I am *so* glad God chose us all to be together on this crazy and wonderful adventure. Dad and I love you with all that we are.

To our parents: Mark and I are forever grateful and indebted to you. We love and honor you today and always. xx

Thank you to our HopeUC family in Australia, and now India and the USA. Ahhhhh . . . where do I start? I love that we do messy, family church. I love that there's always room at the table. I love how you love God's presence. Thank you for trusting Mark and me as we trust and follow Jesus alongside you. What an amazing and miraculous journey!

And thanks to Margie Holmes, the world's most loyal and trusted PA. Thanks also to HopeGlobal and all who continually sacrifice in this space to lift the life of another.

To my new friends at HarperCollins, thanks for your patience with me as I have wrestled out this book. I am completely honored to be doing this season with you all.

To Danny McGuffey and Mark Gilroy, my USA cheer squad and quality control team, thanks for gently guiding me, editing like a boss, continuing to bring me opportunities that blow me away, and for standing by me when life was looking extremely tough and hope was looking very slim. I will always be grateful.

To the team at Integrity Music, what a glorious honor it is to be part of your team.

To my dear friend Joyce Meyer, the fact that you have taken the time to write this foreword and continue to cheer me on in the midst of your ever-expanding world is humbling and extremely appreciated. You are like a spiritual momma to so many, and the fact that you continue to make time for the one just proves that point to me again and again. We love and value you so much!

Thank you to all the pastors and leaders along the way who have encouraged, challenged, loved, and supported us. the churches who have hosted worship nights, and the millions who have sung songs with us as we've praised God from the depth of our beings. What a glorious ride this side of heaven. We are eternally grateful.

And to you, the reader. Thank you for coming on this Golden Thread journey with me. We may never meet but I love how a song or a book, a dance, a melody, a painting, or a photo can actually align our hearts toward a common goal or purpose. I truly pray for you all, that your lives will continue to go from strength to strength as you honor God in and through your entire life, finding the strong, precious strand of His greatness to be the one thing you can always count on.

Please get in touch with me via Instagram @darlenezschech or via my website at darlenezschech.com or follow our tribe at @HopeUC or @Hope_Global.

We'd love to hear from you.

With much love always,
Darlene

NOTES

Chapter 1: God's Presence Is Everything
1. Brother Lawrence, *The Practice of the Presence of God* (Renaissance Classics, 2012), 1, 16.
2. Alicia Britt Chole, *Sitting In God's Sunshine . . . Resting in His Love* (Nashville, TN: J Countryman Books, 2005).

Chapter 2: Seek Him First
1. Robert Robinson, "Come, Thou Fount of Every Blessing," public domain.

Chapter 3: What an Adventure!
1. Jack Hayford, "Preparing for a New 'God-Thing,'" Jack Hayford Ministries, accessed August 13, 2018, https://www.jackhayford.org/teaching/articles/preparing-for-a-new-god-thing/.

Chapter 5: Strength in Weakness
1. Corrie ten Boom, *Tramp for the Lord*, (Grand Rapids, MI: Baker, 1974), 61.
2. Matthew Henry's Commentary on the Bible, Volume IX.

Chapter 6: The Power of The Table
1. Brené Brown, *Daring Greatly* (New York: Avery, 2015), 145,
2. N. T. Wright, *Simply Christian: Why Christianity Makes Sense* (New York: HarperOne, 2006), page 211.

Chapter 7: Transformed by Hope

1. Father Raniero Cantalamessa, *Sober Intoxication of the Spirit: Filled with the Fullness of God*, trans. Marsha Daigle-Williamson (Cincinnati, OH: Servant, 2005).
2. C. S. Lewis, *Mere Christianity* (New York: HarperOne, 1980), 134.

Chapter 9: Forgiveness

1. Excerpted from "I'm Still Learning to Forgive" by Corrie ten Boom. Reprinted by permission from *Guideposts* magazine. Copyright © 1972 by Guideposts Associates, Inc., Carmel, New York 10512.
2. Martin Luther King, Jr., *Letters From the Birmingham Jail* (New York: HarperCollins, 1994).

Chapter 10: Walking in the Spirit

1. Saint Augustine, *On the Holy Trinity; Doctrinal Treatises; Moral Treatises*, trans. A. W. Haddam (Eerdmans, 1872).

Chapter 11: Holy Discontent

1. Malala Yousafzai, "The Nobel Peace Prize Lecture," 2014. Copyright The Nobel Prize. "Malala Yousafzai's Speech at the Youth Takeover of the United Nations," Theirworld.org, July 12, 2013, https://theirworld.org/explainers/malala-yousafzais-speech -at-the-youth-takeover-of-the-united-nations.

Chapter 12: One with Him

1. Rick Warren, *The Purpose Driven Life* (Grand Rapids, MI: Zondervan, 2002), 79.
2. John Piper, "God Is Most Glorified in Us When We Are Most Satisfied in Him," Desiring God, October 13, 2012, https://www.desiringgod.org/messages/ god-is-most-glorified-in-us-when-we-are-most-satisfied-in-him.
3. Wikiquote, s.v. "Irenaeus," accessed August 20, 2018, https:// en.wikiquote.org/wiki/Irenaeus.

Chapter 14: Checks and Balances

1. T. D. Jakes, *Reposition Yourself: Living Life Without Limits* (New York: Atria, 2007), 214.

Chapter 16: Soar

1. Max Lucado, "Our Prayers Do Make a Difference," Crosswalk.com, October 20, 2003, https://www.crosswalk.com/faith/spiritual-life /our-prayers-do-make-a-difference-1225673.html.

ABOUT THE AUTHOR

AUSTRALIAN DARLENE ZSCHECH IS ACCLAIMED ALL OVER THE world as a worship leader, composer, pastor, author, and speaker, and although she has achieved numerous gold albums and her songs are sung in many nations of the world, her family and serving the local church remain Darlene's highest priorities.

Darlene's success simply stands as a testimony to her life's passion for loving God and people with all her heart.

"First and foremost I am a woman who simply and wholeheartedly loves Christ, and serves Him through loving my family, serving the church, and speaking up for those who cannot speak for themselves."

Darlene and Mark are the senior pastors of Hope Unlimited Church (HopeUC) on the Central Coast of New South Wales, Australia, which now also has churches in India and the USA.

Her growing family includes Amy and son-in-law Andrew, Chloe and son-in-law Hosanna, (Darlene calls them "sons-in-love") and Zoe Jewel along with beautiful granddaughters Ava Pearl, Ruthie Feather, and Thea Mae, and grandson Roman Emmanuel Mark.

Connect with Darlene on Facebook, Instagram, and Twitter
@darlenezschech
Website: DarleneZschech.com

MUSIC NOW AVAILABLE FROM

DARLENE ZSCHECH

DARLENE ZSCHECH & HOPEUC

A CHRISTMAS WORSHIP GATHERING